Modelling Integrated Socio-technical Feedback Systems:

e-Democracy and Other Applications

Zach-Amaury Boufoy-Bastick
&
Lenandlar Singh

Modelling Integrated Socio-technical Feedback Systems:

e-Democracy and Other Applications

Zach-Amaury Boufoy-Bastick
&
Lenandlar Singh

University of Guyana
Department of Computer Science

Modelling Integrated Socio-technical Feedback Systems

© 2005 University of Guyana
Department of Computer Science

British Library Cataloguing Publication data
A catalogue record for this book is available from the British Library

ISBN-13   978-976-624-028-8(pbk)
ISBN-10   976-624-028-0 (pbk)

Library of Congress catolog record available

Printed in the United States of America

Boufoy-Bastick, Zach-Amaury
Singh, Lenandlar
Integrated Socio-technical Feedback Systems:
e-Democracy and Other Applications

p. cm.
Includes bibliographical references

This work is dedicated to the principles
and practices of e-democracy

Modelling Integrated Socio-technical Feedback Systems

CONTENTS

Tables

Figures

Introduction

The ideals of open standards and innovative discussion have been central to the development of networked Computer-Mediated Communication technologies. E-mail, Internet Relay Chat, and the World Wide Web have all evolved upon such ideals. Conversely, the products of past and current open development, from the early ARPAnet to the modern web-based forum, force the user into a pre-established world of moderation and socio-technical hierarchies.

This document uses analogies from political science to discuss and analyze the growth of virtual moderation, identifying the four developmental categories of a posteriori moderation, a priori moderation, team moderation, external moderation and self-moderation. This analysis shows that past and current moderation mechanisms strongly contrast with the ideals upon which the development of networked Computer-Mediated Communication technology are based and supports the conclusion that alternative open technologies will now be developed to extend the user base for network development into traditionally less technical disciplines.

Computer-mediated communication technologies which provide for virtual communities have typically evolved in a cross-dichotomous manner, such that technical constructs of the technology have evolved independently from the social environment of the community. The present text analyses some limitations of current implementations of computer-mediated communication technology that are implied by such a dichotomy, and discusses their inhibiting effects on possible developments of virtual communities. A Socio-Technical Indicator Model is introduced that utilizes integrated feedback to describe, simulate and operationalise increasing representation within a variety of structurally and parametrically diverse systems. In illustration, applications of the model are briefly described for financial markets and for eco-systems. A detailed application is then provided to resolve the aforementioned technical limitations of moderation on the evolution of virtual communities. The application parameterises virtual communities to function as self-transforming social-technical systems which are sensitive to emergent and shifting community values as products of on-going communications within the collective. A simulation is presented of the model's application to representative moderation in virtual communities, of which e-democracy is an important sub-class. This simulation demonstrates system conditions for convergence and for status stability of Special Interest Groups that promote differing community values.

Review of CMC
and Moderation

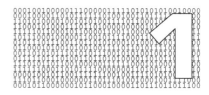

IDENTIFYING FOUR HISTORICAL CATEGORIES OF MODERATION

With few exceptions, computer literature has long described the internet as a democratic plebiscitary arena, allowing for conceptually unrestrained freedom of speech[1]. However, users without the sufficient technical knowledge to form their own virtual communities, write their own protocols or design their own network software are confined to an already sculpted world of virtual moderation and pre-established socio-technical hierarchies. From the early experimental ARPAnet to the contemporary commercial web-based forum, moderation has almost always been a central tenet of virtual communication and, if not always implementing practical restrictions on freedom of speech, certainly has implied controlled communication and

---

[1]   For example, see: Hauben (1997, p.3); Spears and Lee (1994, p.428).

restricted information flow. It should perhaps be noted that literature on the history of computing seems to be predominantly of a technical focus, and that little has been written on the socio-technical history of moderation in computer-mediated communication (CMC). The aim of this study is not to chronicle the application of moderation within every single networked technology, as such an endeavour would be of colossal nature and yet essentially minor in its contribution to the continued development of networked Computer-Mediated Communication. Rather, this study discusses and analyzes moderation techniques and mechanisms within both technological and temporal contexts. This study categorises moderation in networked communication technologies as either a posteriori moderation, team moderation, external moderation or self-moderation. It will, thus, analyse the development of moderation in terms of this categorisation, from the ARPAnet to the modern-day web-based forum.

THE ARPANET: HISTORICAL CONTEXT AND MODERATION

The concept of moderating network communication technology can be traced to the very roots of the internet during the nineteen-sixties and seventies. A strong juxtaposition of hippy freedom and propagandist security seems to have provided the odd, but fertile soil of the internet's growth. It was in the midst of the Cold War that the United States Department of Defence founded the Advanced Research Projects Agency (ARPA) which, in turn, provided funding for one of the first wide-area network communication technologies - the APRAnet. After submitting a two-hundred page proposal, Cambridge (Mass.)-based Bolt, Beranek and Newman (BBN) was contracted for the project. In an October 1967 meeting, ARPA standardised the network (Hauben, 1997, Part I) by setting the technical specification of the Interface Message Processor (IMP), which represented the communication layer of a host. The first IMP was implemented on a SDS SIGMA 7 at the University of California at Los Angeles in 1969, followed shortly after by additional nodes at the Stanford Research Institute, the University of California at Santa Barbara, and the University of Utah (Network Working Group, RFC2235, 1997). By 1977, the ARPAnet was a trans-continental network stretching between Hawaii and Norway, and exceeded fifty hosts in size (Hauben, 1997, p.41). Indeed, the network became the largest wide-area network on the globe, allowing access to individuals from different national backgrounds.

Yet, although the ARPAnet became a geographically 'distributed society', to use Rasmussen's term (Rasmussen, 2003), it was hardly a heterogeneous one. Access to the ARPAnet was provided only to those academic computer science departments with Department of Defense funding (Hauben, 1997, p.42) and to a limited number of companies contracted to the defense industry (Hauben, 1997, p.61). "It was commonly accepted at the time that to join the Arpanet took political connections and $100,000"(cited in Hauben, 2000). Due in large part to the exclusive nature of the network, it required very little moderation. Participants in relatively exclusive community networks can appropriately allocate their attention to the informal social code of the community, thus reducing disruptive posts (Resnick, 2004, p.1). This is not to say, however, that no moderation actually existed. The administrators of an IMP could control its users and moderate their activities, either locally of through the use of a dumb terminal. On the May 3rd, 1978 the Digital Equipment Corporation (DEC) attempted a new sale pitch by widely distributing a commercial ARPAnet message advertising the benefits of their new computer systems - the new DEC-20 and TOPS-20 OS which had ARPAnet software built in. The plethora of addresses were typed in manually and, since SNDMSG limited the amount of space that could be used in the To: field, more addresses were typed in the subject field which, in turn, overflowed into the CC:, and Body: fields - hence many of the intended recipients did not receive the message (Templeton, n/d). Nevertheless, an official ARPA response was issued to the mass-mailing, referring to the message as a "flagrant violation of [the terms of use of] ARPAnet" (cited in Templeton, n/d) and stating that "appropriate action is being taken to preclude its occurrence again" (cited in Templeton, n/d). The official ARPA response was one of the first major moderator actions in computer-mediated network communication technology; it exemplifies what is referred to here as a posteriori moderation, in which messages are moderated only after they are posted. This form of moderation, which was common in earlier computer-mediated communication technologies, moderates for the future use of the technology. To this extent, it is perhaps important to note that the very structure of the ARPAnet limited the form of moderation which could be enacted; that is, since not all messages could go through a central 'moderation' node, messages did not enter an external temporary network in which they could have been edited or discarded before they were posted to the actual ARPAnet. Although it was perhaps feasible to implement such a system at the time, the fact that it was not maturely implemented indicates that such 'moderation' was low on the list of administrative priorities of the time. Later technologies and networks would implement similar types of moderation to that of the ARPAnet, even if more developed moderation mechanisms were internally implemented within the technology. For instance, the NSFnet administrators and the Bulletin Board System (BBS) SysOps, would all come to apply a posteriori moderation. Alternative forms of moderation, particularly a priori moderation, would become implemented with further technologies, such as Netnews.

USENET ABUSE AND MODERATION

This brief historical overview of Usenet abuse and forms of moderation it engendered is now structured and discussed in terms of emergent structures relevant to enhancements and impediments to democratically moderated computer communication vis the emergence of a moderator class, a priori moderation, team moderation, interpretational dilemmas, bias and representative moderation.

In order to provide an alternative to the restrictive limitations of ARPAnet, an open Netnews system, now applied as Usenet, was formed in 1979. Usenet is the result of initial efforts by

Duke University students Tom Truscott and Jim Ellis, and the continuing efforts of a community prepared to offer a more broadly accessible arena of communication. The established telephone network could be used to forward files, thus making the technology independent of costly dedicated lines. Indeed, the financial investment that was needed in order to take part in Usenet was usually limited to that of a computer and a modem. Thus, this allowed for a more demographically open technology, and it would soon became known as the "Poor man's ARPAnet" (Gillespie, 2001, p.9). The original Usenet functioned as a newsletter application which compared timestamps of remote files to those of local files, and transferred any newer files to the local machine using the Unix-to-Unix copy program (UUCP) included within distributions of Unix version 7. This allowed for a networked community to share the newest files on any given machine with every other machine on the network. Following initial complaints from users, Usenet was re-written from Unix Shell to C by Duke University student Stephen Daniel in order to allow for faster execution (Hauben, 1997, p.40). The openness of Usenet allowed for a vast cross-section of opinions, users and discussions.

Due in large part to the heterogeneous nature of Usenet, both in content and in users, the technology saw the birth of built-in moderation apparatus and the emergence of a new socio-technical 'moderator' class. During the Usenet years, moderation shifted from a generally unnecessary act of power enforcement, to an integral aspect of networked communication - the act of which became internally embodied within the privileges of certain users. This shift parallels the popularisation and lowering of entry barriers in computer-mediated communication technology. Indeed, end-user access is essentially free and Usenet eventually grew from under 500 newsgroups in 1988 to over 17,000 in 1996 (Whittaker, et al., n/d, p.1). Besides geographical and linguistic separation, participants often differed in their goals and needs, each of which shapes the final participation of a user in a newsgroup (Golder, 2003, p.iii). Yet, perhaps the heterogeneous nature of Usenet is best illustrated through the emergence of multiple news hierarchies and delivery structures. Newsgroups are clustered into hierarchies, each hierarchy representing a different field of interest. Further, delivery structures exist such that Usenet allows for Announce groups; Binary groups; Digests; Discussion groups and Source groups - with each structure attracting varying forms of discussion or, as is often the case, argument, and thus applying varying degrees of moderation. Announce groups, for example, are used to distribute announcements about related newsgroups and have a fast turnaround time; thus requiring only light moderation (Landfield, 2001, module 6.1). Discussion groups, however, often become taverns for heated arguments and inappropriate posts, and thus generally apply heavier moderation (Landfield, 2001, module 6.4). Although Usenet developed alongside a philosophy of internal moderation mechanisms, the free exchange of ideas remains a central tenet of the technology. Communities can form their own groups, in which their own Acceptable Use Policy is applied. Disgruntlement with a groups Policy from any set of users is balanced by the ability of a user to seek a new community or form their own. The result of such an approach is that moderation has been an optional path for localised Usenet communities rather than a bureaucratic control of the general network[2]. Indeed, the network represents a printing press of the individual and the forum of the community. Hence, it should be noted that moderation in the Usenet environment has not evolved to advance censorship and certainly did not restrict the direct publication of ideas or opinions in a network-wide context. Instead, moderation in Usenet acts as a power of organisation, format sanitisation, and superficial editing.

Although the general Usenet network provides freedom of expression for the community, moderated newsgroups in particular resemble academic journals more than they do social forums. Moderated newsgroups apply a priori moderation, in which moderators review, and sometimes edit, posts before deciding whether they should be submitted or discarded. The first moderated newsgroup appeared in 1984, for the purpose of isolating administrative posts from opinion and gossip (Sansom, 1995, p.6). Yet the purpose of moderating newsgroups is multifaceted. Groups with a high content volume use moderation to reduce the load of the newsgroup, groups which are meant as formal information outlets are moderated in order to insure distribution by a select few, and groups which suffer from abuse are moderated in order to reduce such abuse

---

[2]   The freedom that the void of bureaucratic control implies was appreciated in the early 1980s as it is appreciated today; See: 1983 Post on CSNET, Hauben, 1997, p.199.

(Landfield, 2001, module 3). However, even though individual moderated groups generally provide an Acceptable Use Policy or a Charter, moderation is subject to the moderator's interpretation of both the Charter and the posts of the group. Participants to newsgroups, being heterogeneous as a whole, differ of opinion individually, and what is thus considered moderation to one may easily be considered censorship to another. Activities such as trolling, flaming, spamming, and flooding, for instance, benefit some whilst impeding others (Lampe, 2004, p.1). Flaming, for instance, may allow one to openly express their emotions, but in doing so decreases message structure (Mabry, 1996), thus fettering the interpretation of the flame's recipients. Similarly, lurking may satisfy the personal and informational needs of a user whilst acting as a hindrance to public participation and as overhead (Nonnecke, & Preece, 2000). Yet, it is the role of the moderator, usually of a single conscience, to decide for the benefit of the entire community. Hence, although the Charter of a community may be decided upon democratically, its application is subject to the absolute interpretation of the moderator. In general, computer-mediated technology lacks many of the traditional characteristics upon which effective communication depends, such as complex systems of real-time mutual adjustment and correction (Riva, 2001, p.205); Since the very nature of Usenet provides an environment where fewer linguistic cues are afforded (at least relative to a non-virtual environment), interpretation difficulties are augmented, and these difficulties become inherent to Usenet moderation. Furthermore, in cases where there are too few moderators for a heavy load newsgroup, freedom of speech is often sacrificed for the efficient moderation process. Thus, in an effort to democratize the moderation system, a few newsgroups apply 'team moderation' in which moderation is applied through the decisions of a group. The sci.med.aids group, created on June 13, 1987, applied such a form of moderation. Moderators of the group, maintaining distinct roles such as 'chief moderator' or 'expert contributor', communicated via electronic mail in order to reach consensus on issues of moderation (Greening, 1988, p.1). Amongst further benefits[3] such as efficiency, well-formed team moderation allows for a more representative moderation team: one which reflects the opinions of both the majority and the marginalized subsection of the community. However, badly-formed team moderation may be no more representative than individual moderation since, as Benjamin Franklin so eloquently wrote in 1787, "when you assemble a number of men to have the advantage of their joint wisdom you inevitably assemble with those men, all their prejudices, their passions, their errors of opinion, their local interests, and their selfish views" (Farrand p. 642). Hence, given that any team of moderators is jointly biased, the benefits of team moderation may lie exclusively in efficiency and exclude representation of the community. Although a posteriori moderation would largely remain standard for technologies to come, the maturing of internal moderation mechanisms of web-based forums merits some discussion within the context of this paper.

---

[3]   For statements on the additional benefits of team moderation, See: Greening (1988, pp.6-9) and Landfield (2001, module 10).

WEB-BASED FORUMS: HISTORICAL REVIEW AND MODERATION

Upon the infrastructure provided by an evolved ARPAnet, grew a new layer of communication technology called the World Wide Web (hereafter referred to as 'the Web'). Tim Berners-Lee at the 'Centre Européen pour la Recherche Nucléaire' (CERN) developed the Web in 1991 in order to integrate systems and standardize access interfaces, whilst providing an automated way to navigate from one resource to another. Navigation would occur through the traversal of links (Berners-Lee, 1990), based upon Ted Nelson's research on 'hypertext' (Berners-Lee, 1996). In order to perform such tranversal, Berners-Lee wrote the first native web browser application, called 'WorldWideWeb', in 1990. The browser was hardware limited, being only able to run on 'Next' machines, which were not commonly distributed at the time (Berners-Lee, n/d) and, although it did admittedly provide a Graphical User Interface, the browser window was unable to draw in-line graphical objects. In an effort to lower access boundaries, Nicola Pellow wrote a 'line mode' browser which was portable to multiple platforms. The Erwise, Viola, Cello and Mosaic browsers followed, and graphical rendering would eventually become available with the release of Pei Wei's Viola in 1992. Despite a plethora of varied and collectively contradictory statistics on internet growth[4], it would seem that traffic on

---

[4]   Internet growth statistics differ dramatically from each other and are collectively contradictory. A 1998 report by the United States Commerce Department on "The Emerging Digital Economy", states that internet traffic doubles every 100 days (Margherio et al., 1998, p.8), whereas contemporary ... cont

internet backbones has steadily doubled annually (Odlyzko, 2003). The popular explosion of the internet may well be linked to that of the desktop computer in the mid-90s (Follman, 2001, p.71) and to an adherence to open standards, such as HTTP and TCP/IP, defined by the World Wide Web Consortium and the Internet Society (Berners-Lee, 1996; Follman, 2001, pp.77-79). This openness was paralleled in the domain of content, as the Web allowed for the interconnection of multiple types of documents and resources, from simple text files to legacy system databases. In essence, a user has the ability to weave content of their choosing onto the web. This provides an intrinsic freedom of speech to the developer and webmaster; for the user, however, limitations are imposed by the fruits of the prior.

With the common adoption of graphical environments and the success of the desktop computer, the web has allowed for the mass-popularization of new web-based computer-mediated communication technologies, such as the web-based forum (hereafter forum). The forum stems from Usenet and, at least in the context of moderation, generally suffers from the same

---

… analysts state more modest figures of internet traffic doubling every year (Odlyzko, 2003). Discrepancies exist for a multitude of reasons including differences in sampling methodology (Tehan, 2002, pp.1-2), lack of consistent records (Coffman, et al., 2000) and confusion between capacity and usage. Retrospectively, commercial estimates of internet growth seem to have been largely inflated, as indicated by estimates that only 2.7% of lit fiber capacity in the United States is currently in use (Dreazen, 2002).

restrictions as newsgroups. Moderator interpretation, ambiguous Acceptable Use Policies, collectively biased and unrepresentative moderator classes, for instance, are moderation complications which are shared amongst newsgroups and forums. Even so, differences do exist, particularly in that a more explicit socio-technical hierarchy is applied in web-based forums. Some popular forums even apply a social ranking system based on post-counts or other criteria. An example of such a forum is the popular open-source phpBB forum software (phpBB, n/d, p.29). Such ranking systems have few technical implications for the user[5], but rather aid in the establishment of a well-defined social hierarchy. In the specific case of phpBB, for instance, user ranks can be created simply by selecting users to fill those ranks, rather than necessitating that certain user-specific conditions be realized (phpBB, n/d, p.28). Ranked users are separated from the rest of the community through special titles and avatar images (phpBB, n/d, p.29). The socio-technical forum hierarchy traditionally consists of a legislative administrator class and an executive moderator class. Generally easy-to-use moderation mechanisms are built-in to web-based forums, allowing for such extreme actions as banning members to be a simple point and click process. When

---

[5]   Exceptions do exist, such as the applied use of post count and rank in order to allow access to certain private sections of a forum. Moreover, a similar user segregation mechanism, called 'grouping', allows users certain access privileges on specific forums; being a member of a private group hence entitles the user to view and post in forums that non-group members would not have access to (phpBB, n/d, pp.11-12).

banned, users are socially outcast from their communities and must seek new communities. However, technical possibilities exist to undermine this social restriction. Users can, for instance, be reintegrated into a community, at least on a technical outset, through the creation of new pseudonyms, the switching of Internet Protocol addresses and spoofing methods (Dahlberg, 2001b). Yet such circumvention techniques are perhaps better suited to the technically advanced user which privileges what tends to be technical discussion over humanistic discussion, since this administrative moderation mechanism is still effective in humanistic interest communities which tend to lower levels of technical understanding or exposure.

UNIVERSAL MECHANISM OF SELF-MODERATION: DE-INDIVIDUALIZATION, NETIQUETTE, FORMAL AND INFORMAL ENFORCEMENT OF DISCOURSE DECORUM

Common to many web-based forums, newsgroups and chat systems is the user-level implementation of self-moderation. We define self-moderation as the conscious and intentional effort of a user to moderate his or her own discourse prior to contributing to a community. Large-scale virtual communities often provide arenas of communication wherein interlocutor identity is blurred. In face-to-face communication, a person's social identity is embodied within the physical character of that person, anchoring their identity and stabilizes conversation (Donath, 1998, p.1). Yet the virtual world of large-scale communication is largely a textual and disembodied one. A consequence of the predominantly textual nature of computer-mediated communication is that user names appear simply as text. There is no guarantee that such usernames truly represent the intended recipient of conversation (Riva, 2001). In such cases where users are represented by aliases, non-virtual personal relevance is bypassed. The formation of such pseudo-names makes it difficult for users to correlate the social identities of others with their technical name representation; it is not necessarily a simple task for a user to create an identity around a text-based name. Compounding the inherent lack of technical identity representation, chat technologies provide environments wherein it may be difficult to maintain coherent and sustained topical conversation. Internet Relay Chat, for example, represents conversation in sequential lines of text; such structure difficultly accommodates multiple, yet concurrent, conversations within the same communication space. Indeed, the turn-taking that is traditionally found in oral communication is complicated in these environments (Riva, 2001); such loss of conversational flow often leads to chaotic conversation and further minimizes identity correlation. As personal responsibility is not easily attributed in such situations, users tend to more liberal discourse[6] such as flaming. Yet the correlation between discourse style and privacy does not lend itself as a direct practical solution to minimizing

---

[6]   See: McKenna and Bargh (2000, pp.60-62) for the attribution of increased self-disclosure to de-individualisation on the internet; Joinson (2001) study for association of increased self-disclosure and lower self-awareness to computer-mediated communication.

abuse; personally identifying and tracking users as a means of moderation would not only be a technical and bureaucratic complication but, even more importantly, threaten the foundational 'freedom of speech' tenet upon which much of the appeal of networked technologies is based. Perhaps the Netherlands National Commission for UNESCO, in advising on State internet moderation and human rights, wrote it best:

> "...privacy is an indispensable prerequisite to the right of freedom of expression and the right to communicate. Online as well as offline, readers, listeners and viewers have a right to the same high level of privacy and anonymity. If online access to information is tracked and tied to detailed personal profiles, self censorship is imminent and - more important still - the public debate and the rule of law are eroded." (UNESCO NL, 2005, p.2)

In order to minimize abuse without threatening either privacy or freedom of speech, online communities have established norms of discourse that are collectively named netiquette. Netiquette rules, such as those outlined by Rinaldi (1998), provide generally accepted policy as well as subtle local community convention, which users are expected to observe during discourse. These rules generally attempt to promote social controls in order to protect the community from reproachable conduct, such as ethical violations, bandwith wastage and inappropriate or deliberatly hostile language (Papadakis, 2003, p.32). At least to the extent of netiquette, it is the responsibility of the user to moderate his or her discourse within a community's conversation space. Capitalizing an entire line of text is considered contrary to netiquette, as is indiscriminate cross-posting in a Usenet environment (Whittaker, et al., n/d, p.1). Yet, as noted above, individual communities expect local, and sometimes subtle, rules of decorum; for instance, whereas flaming is generally considered breach of netiquette, alt.flaming encourages the activity (Kollock and Smith, 1996).

In the specific case of Minnesota E-Democracy, adherence to local conversation conventions has been relatively successful (Dahlberg, 2001a). Netiquette is enforced actively and informally through peer pressure, such as public reproaches from high-ranking members or criticism through private e-mail (Papadakis, 2003, p.33). Yet formal, in-active mechanisms of enforcement also exist. Some forums and discussion lists, for instance, attempt to discourage lurking by suggesting in their guidelines that new users should introduce themselves to the community (Nonnecke et, & Preece, 2000, p. 6). Yet, despite the existence of Frequently Asked Questions and Acceptable Use Policies which contain nettetique guidelines, rules of conversation are sometimes ignored by community interlocutors. Indeed, the very documents stating discourse decorum are often ignored by discussion participants (Kollock, & Smith, 1996). Cross-posting, for instance, is highly frequent in Usenet newsgroups (Whittaker, et al., n/d, p.6). Hence, moderators may nevertheless regulate user postings within a formally moderated environment. Moderators may hence kick guests from IRC channels, @boot users from MUDs, ban users on web-based forums, or invoke a 'cancel-bot' to identify and remove violator postings on Usenet. Further, automated programs may scan for technical netiquette violations, such as over-capitalization or extremely long messages, and edit or discard the posts appropriately. This saves human moderation effort and time. In such cases where moderator-level intervention fails, a user may implement alternative forms of self-moderation, such as content-based or semantic filtering. Multiple newsreaders offer the functionality of a 'kill-file', the user-level equivalent of a cancel-bot, which can be used to remove posts given specific criterion. Self-moderation mechanisms such as adherence to netiquette and the filtering discussed above, allow for personal and community sensitivity whilst maintaining the anonymity that allows users to express their true opinions, free of concerns of self-presentation (Spears, & Lea, 1994, p. 430). It is hence an appropriate alternative to external moderation for the responsible user, and a convenient filter against abuse of the irresponsible or malicious user.

CONCLUSION

As Cain contends in his paper on internet democracy, "internet technology is neither inherently democratic nor tyrannical" (Cain, n/d, p. 1005). As this study has shown through a discussion and analysis of moderation mechanisms, the moderated communication technologies present on the internet dictate the environments of users, in effect forcing users into a pre-established socio-technical hierarchies and moderation systems. It is, hence, the inherent nature of current moderated computer-mediated communication technology to lend itself to the political equivalents of absolutism or oligarchy. As Papadakis states, "computer-mediated environments are not necessarily egalitarian or inclusive" (Papadakis, 2003, p. 36), and so Internet Relay Chat and web-based forums, for instance, implement socio-technical hierarchies. As this study has discussed, the practice of ranking members of the community is even a technical possibility offered in web-based forums; and since purely social rankings are sometimes technically represented, it would seem that hierarchy has evolved to serve purposes beyond that of pure moderation. A radical dichotomy thus appears when we compare democratic communication of the internet of old, specifically the ARPAnet and early Usenet, with that of the contemporary internet. Yet conversely, the internet has evolved upon the ideals of open standards and innovative discussion, albeit within specialised fields: E-mail, Internet Relay Chat, and the World Wide Web all evolved to serve democratic communicative needs of the user community.

In concluding, we propose that it may be appropriate to unshackle this continuing ideal of flexible communication from the development of applied technologies that promote absolutist and oligarchist moderated communications, and provide the technological developments for a wider voicing of community opinions and a more open development of non-technical thought. Such technological developments will help users to collectively control their communities, protecting shunned users from abusive rule and the need to seek exile within more socio-technically representative moderated forums. It is the responsibility of the Computer Scientist and the programmer to allow for more democratic computer-mediated communication technology. The development of such technology could realise the incredible potential that network communication now offers.

Framework of the Socio-Technical Indicator Model

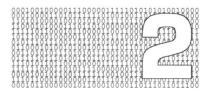

WHY THE STI MODEL WAS DEVELOPED

In recent years, a growing literature has emerged on interest-oriented relationship systems within virtual communities (Li, 2004). Yet, although much research has been conducted on interactions within such communities, and on their impact to their external society, little has been published on how representatively the virtual community structures reflect the social structure of the external community. Indeed, computer-mediated communication technologies, which provide for virtual communities, have typically evolved in a cross-dichotomous manner, with technical constructs of the technology evolving independently from the social environment of the community. Hence, technical mechanisms of virtual community, such as moderation, are generally insensitive to the social structures within the communities in which they operate. Such technical mechanisms have come to depend heavily upon the external agency of community members to sensitize the socio-technical environment of the virtual community. As this study will evidence, these social-technological limitations have typically resulted in virtual communities having to use inflexible unrepresentative communication environments which have, in turn, limited their evolution and restricted their options for growth. In order to resolve these limitations, a Socio-Technical Indicator Model has been developed that simulates generalized integrated community feedback systems. The general model is presented and shown to have applications to structurally and parametrically diverse systems as varied as financial markets and eco-systems. Finally, the model is applied to the moderation function of virtual communities, resolving traditional limitations by operationalising the virtual community as a self-transforming social-technical system, sensitive to emergent values as products of on-going communications within the collective.

BACKGROUND OF PREVIOUS CMC MODELS

Mechanisms of moderation and representations of user status are two inherent concepts of virtual community, each of which has generally evolved independently of the other. A categorisation that is sensitive to this dichotomy can be assumed, such that the prior is viewed as a technical concept and the latter as a social concept. However, this is a crossed dichotomy in that moderation has typically evolved as a technical component which operates a priori on the social environment in which it is applied and, conversely, status representation is largely a social component, which typically has implied little bearing on the technical workings of the community. In order to contextualise this crossed dichotomy, a background review of moderation mechanisms and status representation, which illustrates this crossed dichotomy by their respective sensitivities and flexibilities to the communities they have served, is now presented.

In itself, moderation has typically been restricted to the political science equivalents of absolutism or oligarchy. That is, throughout the evolution of virtual communities, moderation has generally been the responsibility of individuals within the community, selected through circumstance or relationship rather than as functions of the community itself. Perhaps, the earliest instance of such moderation occurred over the ARPAnet, the first wide-area network funded by the Department of Defence's Advanced Research Projects Agency (ARPA). This network, which started as a single Interface Message Processor node at the University of California at Los Angeles in 1969, eventually grew to include nodes at the Stanford Research Institute, the University of California at Santa Barbara, and the University of Utah (Zakon, RFC2235, 1997). Due in part to the largely homogeneous and exclusive nature of its users, moderation existed as an informal and ill-defined function. Although no technically-defined moderator class was established within the early ARPAnet, the role was fulfilled, at least on one occasion, by ARPA officials[7]. Hence, ARPAnet moderation was an informal

---

[7]   For instance, ARPA formally responded to the Digital Equipment
       Corporation's commercial mass-mailing ... cont

property of an institutional affiliation. Later, through an evolutionary shift paralleled by the lowering of entry boundaries and the popularisation of computer-mediated communication, a moderator class became an inherent component of synchronous systems, such as Internet Relay Chat, as well as of asynchronous systems, such as Netnews and modern-day web-based forums. Usenet saw the birth of the built-in moderation apparatus which, unlike the ARPAnet, offered a formal mechanism of moderation for localised communities. Now, modern-day web based forums also offer similar formal moderation mechanisms.

In post-ARPAnet communication spaces, the translation of social values to technical moderation was achieved, to a certain extent, by the adoption of norms of discourse, collectively referred to as netiquette. Netiquette rules, such as those outlined by Rinaldi (1998), provide generally accepted policy as well as subtle local community conventions, which users are expected to observe during discourse. Communities generally provide an Acceptable Use Policy, or a Charter containing netiquette rules for their members to observe. The burden of moderation is, hence, extended to interlocutors within conversation spaces. For example, users within a Usenet environment may be expected

---

.... of May 3rd, 1978 - referring to it as a "flagrant violation of [the terms of use of] ARPAnet" (cited in Templeton, n/d) and stating that "appropriate action is being taken to preclude its occurrence again" (cited in Templeton, n/d).

to avoid capitalizing an entire line of text or indiscriminately cross-posting (Whittaker, et al., n/d, p.1). Nevertheless, such discourse decorum is often ignored by discussion participants (Kollock, & Smith, 1996). Cross-posting, for instance, is frequent in Usenet newsgroups (Whittaker, et al., n/d, p.6). In cases where breaches of netiquette do occur, community moderators are typically burdened with editing the post or contribution. Even so, whether moderation occurs on an interlocutor basis or a moderator basis, guidance by netiquette implies a heavy dependence upon the interpretation of Acceptable Use Policies and Charters. However, this necessary reliance on interpretation is fettered by the very nature of virtual environments. For example, in wide-area systems such as Internet Relay Chat, where concurrent conversations may occur within the same conversation space, messages are, however, displayed in a sequential order. Hence, it may be difficult for users to maintain coherent and sustained topical conversations.

Virtual communication generally also denies interlocutors the use of the social cues which have central regulatory functions in face-to-face communication. In contrast to face-to-face communication, where social meanings of an interlocutor's identity are embodied within their communication acts, the virtual world of large-scale communication is largely a textual and disembodied one. Hence, some of the mechanisms which traditionally anchor identity and stabilize conversation are not present within virtual communication spaces. Within such a context, it is not always appropriate to rely upon individuals, generally of a single conscience, to moderate for the benefit of the entire community. Instead, a few communities apply 'team moderation' in which a sub-section of the community moderates for the entire community. The sci.med.aids group, created on June 13, 1987, applied such a form of moderation. Moderators of the group, maintaining distinct roles such as 'chief moderator' or 'expert contributor', communicated via electronic mail in order to reach consensus on issues of moderation (Greening, 1988, p.1). Among further benefits[8] such as efficiency, well-formed team moderation allows for more representative moderation systems which can reflect the opinions of both the majority and marginalized subsections of the community. Conversely, badly-formed team moderation may be no more representative than individual moderation since, as Benjamin Franklin so eloquently wrote "when you assemble a number of men to have the advantage of their joint wisdom you inevitably assemble with those men, all their prejudices, their passions, their errors of opinion, their local interests, and their selfish views" (cited in Farrand, 1937, p. 642).

Given that any team of moderators can be jointly biased by excluding representation of their community, the benefits of team moderation may lie exclusively in its efficiency. Thus, although netiquette rules may be democratically formulated by the community, the interpretation of the rules may be fettered by the nature of the medium of communication or through collective bias. More importantly, however, is that community

---

[8] For statements on the additional benefits of team moderation, See: Greening (1988, pp.6-9) and Landfield (2001, module 10).

norms and decorum are external to the technical existence of the communication media. This dichotomy between social standards and technical moderation may restrict flexibility; that is, virtual communities may become severely limited in their capacity to evolve, in that they can only evolve by the external agency of human administrators. For instance, in situations where the focus and interest of the general community shifts, whilst the focus and interest of the moderators does not, or where social changes are not paralleled by changes in Charter, virtual communities are denied the flexibility of evolution.

In order to increase social sensitivity within communication technology, many communities technically value 'user contribution' as a direct equivalent of the social construct of user status. For instance, a few popular forums apply a social ranking system based on user post-counts or other criteria. In such systems, wherein posts are generally statically-valued (i.e. where each post is assigned a constant value), a user's status is defined as the sum-value of all their posts. An example of such a forum is the popular, open-source, phpBB forum software (phpBB, n/d, p.29). Such ranking systems have few technical implications for the user[9], but rather aid in the establishment of

---

[9] Exceptions do exist, such as the applied use of post count and rank in order to allow access to certain private sections of a forum. Moreover, a similar user segregation mechanism, called 'grouping', allows users certain access privileges on specific forums; being a member of a private group hence entitles the user to view and post in forums that non-group members would not have access to (phpBB, n/d, pp.11-12).

a technically-represented social hierarchy. In building socio-technical hierarchies, other communities distinguish between various types of contribution and value each type separately. In a study of the music-oriented WholeNote and ActiveBass communities, Kelly, Sung, and Farnham (2002) notes that 'point totals' are assigned to members based upon their contributions. Point totals are incremented by set values based upon the nature of a contribution. For example, 'publishing a lesson' increments a user's point total by ten points, whereas creating a 'home page' increments a member's point total by twenty points (Kelly, et al., 2002, p. 394). A user's point total reflects their membership status within the community, consistent with the implied community value that 'more productive members being more highly considered'. Indeed, such a system may increase contribution as users' ability to influence the community increases the sense of community that any user feels within the virtual environment (Blanchard, & Markus, 2003), and such an ability may be associated with content contribution.

The Slashdot model employs a similar system, at least to the extent that comment descriptors, such as 'off topic' or 'insightful', each correspond to a set positive or negative unitary value (Lampe, & Resnick, 2004, p. 2). Yet, as with the static-valuing functions of popular web-based forums, this is a functional model for these specific communities and cannot easily be generalised to serve values of other communities. For instance, not all communities may provide home pages to their members, and those which do may not consider the creation of a homepage to be worth twenty points. More importantly, however, is the dilemma of how one initially chooses a concrete value, such as 'twenty-points', and who should make such a decision about valuing the resources of an entire community. Further, the model suffers from the same restrictions on flexibility as Netiquette-based moderated communities, since the resource valuing function is external to the social state of the community.

Moderator interpretation, ambiguous Acceptable Use Policies, collectively biased and unrepresentative moderator classes and the creation of socio-technical hierarchies based on inflexible resource-valuing functions are complications which are typically shared amongst current virtual community models. The underlying characteristic of these communities, at least within the context of moderation, is that social constructs are rarely combined with technical constructs but, rather, social environments evolve around the community's technology. In communities where such constructs are combined, external human agency generally acts as a bridge between the technical workings of the forum and its social environment, and, as illustrated, the technology is generally neither sensitive nor flexible to the evolving social states of the communities it serves.

MAPPING COMMUNITY FUNCTIONS TO USER STATUS

In order to provide for more technically sensitive and flexible developments of virtual communities, it is appropriate to provide an operational socio-technical model that merges social and technical constructs of community environments. Within this context, community functions can be shifted from purely peripheral social constructs, such as externally valuing community resources, selecting usage decorum or assigning privileges based upon relationship or circumstance, to technical constructs which are representative of the social state of the community. In order to create such generally applicable sensitive and flexible technology, any single social characteristic of a community that can be evaluated, assessed and valued, should be capable of an isometric mapping to a related technical function and parameter of the model.

Thus, technical functions should allow for sensitive and flexible simulations of community functions that maintain moderator privileges only to the extent that they promote community values. For instance, moderators burdened with classifying contributions in a humour-oriented community should be positively valued by the community for their ability to classify types of humour. These values can be gathered from contributions or processes. Further, if the community's perception of the moderators' ability to classify humour degrades over time, to such an extreme point where the moderator is no longer viewed as socially fit for such a position, then their technical privileges should be removed or the moderator should be replaced. This presents two possibilities for moderator assignment. Firstly, moderator privileges related to a valued social characteristic could be assigned to any willing members of the community, who have the highest status for that characteristic. Secondly, moderators could be assigned in a typical external fashion - through the agency of community members. In either of these cases, the system remains flexible and allows for community evolution in that moderators must satisfy the community, thus providing a minimum level of perceived benefit or value, in order to retain their privileges. Central to the realisation of such a system, is a model which allows for sensitive representation of community satisfaction, resource value and user status.

COMMUNITY CHARACTERISTICS AND THEIR EVALUATION

Virtual communities differ in focus and, consequently, do not all value common characteristics, such as resources and aspects of participation, in the same manner. Activities such as trolling, flaming, spamming, and flooding benefit some whilst impeding others (Lampe, 2004, p.1). Flaming, for instance, may allow the open expression of emotions, but in doing so decrease message structure (Mabry, 1996), thus fettering the interpretation of the flame's recipients. Similarly, lurking may satisfy the personal and informational needs of a user whilst acting as a hindrance to public participation and as system overhead (Nonnecke, & Preece, 2000). In addition to multiple forms of user participation existing individually within a virtual community, specific communities might value one characteristic of participation more than another. An official news outlet, for example, might favor postings by only privileged members and thus encourage general lurking, whereas a community based upon academic discussion might favor deliberative discourse and debate. In building a status-oriented virtual community based upon valued aspects of participation, one hence has to consider a valuing function for various aspects of participation. Computer Science studies have, generally, adopted a defeatist solution of valuing aspects of participation a priori to the community. In a theoretical study on community activity level, for instance, (Barry, et al., 2003, p.4) state that "a community derives little or no value from a user who simply reads messages". Other studies, such as (Ludford, et al., 2004), avoid the complication altogether by operationally defining participation as being only 'visible content contribution'. Furthermore, opinion of resource value may differ between members of a community. For example, Cosley, et al.(2005), in meta-commenting on their study, state that "...we called a newbie question a low-value contribution. But for the asker, for lurkers with the same question, and for members who want to demonstrate their knowledge, the contribution has high value" (Cosley, et al., 2005, p.19). Since opinion of resource value differs amongst, and within, communities, it is inappropriate to adopt an a priori approach to valuing contribution in a generalized community model. Rather, a generalized community model must allow options for systematically rating contributions and valuing individual users with respect to valued social characteristics, in some cases taking into account the values of individual members and special interest groups (SIGs) within the community.

The social environment of a community is likely to comprise multiple social characteristics. Hence, simulation functions are identified in order to evaluate assessable attributes that relate to community. In a technical context, the value of an attribute can be a property of a user contribution, such as length of a post, or it can be a property of user participation, such as the time between posts. In relation to contribution-specific attributes, for example, a given community may wish to measure the attribute of 'contribution quality' in order to modifying user status. In a study of Lotus Notes databases, Whittaker (1996) qualitatively identified computable aspects of virtual discourse. Specifically, he identified 'mean conversational thread length', 'Mean percentage of dead-end conversations', 'Mean Browsing (read/write ratio)' and 'Read Rate (mean reads/day)' as valuable measures of conversation quality (Whittaker, 1996, p.415). These measures lend themselves not only to Whittaker's 'conversation quality' but also, through an associative connection, to the quality of posts by users, as well as to other measures of user contribution. Any other measurable characteristic of discourse, such as aggressiveness or level of profanity, could also be adopted by an implementation of the model. In terms of user processes, a community that is conscious of lurkers might find it appropriate to identify the time between user posts, or the frequency of users' posts, as measurable attributes of participation. From such foundational attributes, it is possible to build an interconnected technical representation of the community's values which determine its social structure, vis-à-vis both community values and user values.

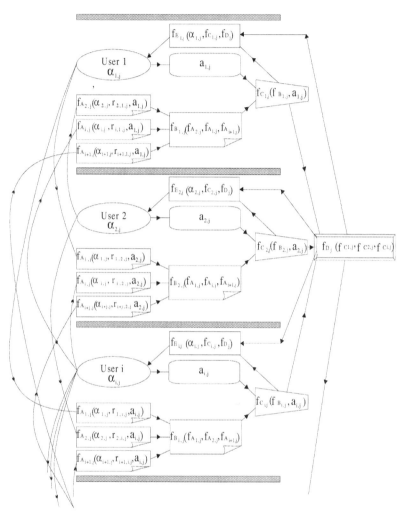

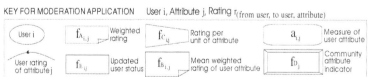

Figure 1: Conceptual Framework of the Socio-Technical Indicator Model

CONCEPTUAL FRAMEWORK OF THE GENERAL SOCIO-TECHNICAL INDICATOR MODEL

The conceptual framework for the general Socio-Technical Indicator Model is illustrated in Figure 1, in which a generalised characteristic of the community j is measured within the community. The model can be viewed as a feedback system, in which a user value, such as status or wealth, is altered through direct and indirect effects of system components. The high-level effects which define the Socio-Technical Indicator Model are illustrated in the meta-model, presented in Figure 2. In order to maintain generalizability, six formulae are used, each of which can be defined so as to simulate various characteristics of representative systems. Indeed, the model is capable of simulating many systems, including financial systems (e.g. stock markets, commercial sales, etc.), bio-conservation systems (e.g. species evolution, wildlife extinction, etc.) and moderation systems for virtual communities. Whilst the application of the model to these systems is detailed in Table 4 and a brief explanation of each application follows, the focus of this discussion will remain on applications to moderation.

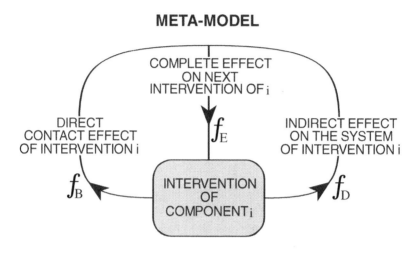

Figure 2: Socio-Technical Indicator Meta-Model

Applications to Moderation

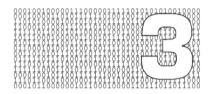

PARAMETERS AND FUNCTIONS

Within the context of moderation, a social characteristic is technically represented by a measurable attribute, j. Hence, the generalised user, User i, is associated with a measure, $a_{i,j}$, for any attribute j. For instance, if j is the 'profanity', then $a_{i,j}$ represents the actual count of occurrences of profanity within User i's contribution. Opinions of the measure $a_{i,j}$, are then collected as ratings from other users and weighted by their respective status, or $\alpha_{i,j}$, which is dubbed the *user socio-technical indicator* for User i and the attribute j. Each $\alpha_{i,j}$ is iteratively modified by both the weighted ratings which the User i receives for their measure of attribute j (e.g. how much the community values their contribution or processes) and by the community's general rating of the attribute j. The community's general rating of attribute j, or its popularity, is dubbed as the *community socio-technical indicator*, or β_j.

Table 1:

Parameters and Functions of
an Application to Moderation

Parameters		Descriptor	Functions	Descriptor	Formulea
System parameters	i	User	$f_{Ai,j}$	Weighted rating	αr
	j	Valued attribute	$f_{Bi,j}$	Average community value of contribution from user i	$\overline{r}_{ai,j} = \dfrac{\sum\limits_{i=1\ldots i-1}^{i+1\ldots n} \alpha_{i,j} r_{i,j}}{n-1}$
Internal parameters	α_i	Status of user i	$f_{Ci,j}$	Average community value per occuence of contribution	$m_{i,j} = \dfrac{\overline{r}_{ai,j}}{a_{i,j}}$
	a	Number of occurences of attribute	$f_{Di,j}$	Popularity of attribute	$\beta_j = HM_i(m_{i,j})$
	$r_{i,j}$	Rating of attribute	$f_{Ei,j}$	Change in status	$f = \dfrac{m_{i,j}}{\beta_j} \times \dfrac{a_{i,j}}{a_j} \times s$

CALCULATING THE COMMUNITY SOCIO TECHNICAL INDICATOR

Both the user socio-technical indicator $\alpha_{i,j,}$ and, therefore, the community socio-technical indicator $\beta_{j,}$ that is derived from the $\alpha_{i,j}$, are manipulated by the weighted ratings of attribute j. This application of the model assumes the use of a double-anchored rating scale, similar to Osgood's Semantic Differential Scale from -5 to +5. Ratings are weighted with user status in relation to an attribute, such that users with a higher status for a given attribute have more effect on valuing an attribute than have users with lower status. Various methods of determining ratings, initially setting user weightings for these ratings, and of combining weightings and ratings, simulate various characteristics of representative systems. For example, where all weightings are set to equal value (e.g. $\alpha_{i,j} = 1$) represents equal valued rating system. Additionally, equally valuing all ratings (e.g. $r_{i,j} = 1$) simulates a 'one man, one vote' system[10]. Otherwise, in an initially hierarchical system, administrators or moderators could be assigned higher ratings than non-privileged users. Variable ratings may be collected through a user interfaced polling system associated with individual posts or, alternatively, defined on a community level.

The actual formula used in this application of the conceptual framework is to weight the rankings with user socio-technical indicators through multiplication. This requires that $\alpha_{i,j} \geq 1$, as any product where this is not the case would distort the average rating data by reducing it. In such a situation, a user's status would be reduced by including zero, or near zero, terms in the divisor of the average calculation, thus counter-intuitively implying that status is reduced by a contribution that encourages many ratings from low status users. It should be noted that deducing alternative formulas to the ones provided herein are possible extensions to research; a simple addition formula, for instance, would measure the popularity of an attribute's measure, rather than its mean rating. Indeed, there are six steps

---

[10]   In such a scenario, an alternative to the 'mean weighted rating' formula, which is presented in the conceptual framework, is needed. Otherwise, outcomes will always be equal to 1.

in the model where formulae are used and each of these is an opportunity to develop finer distinctions of flexible and representatively-moderated virtual communities.

The mean weighted rating, $\bar{r}$, is divided by the measure of the attribute so as to provide the ratio of average weighted weighting per occurrence of the attribute, or a scalar $m_{i,j}$ which indicates the general weighted rating of each single occurrence in a - that is, the measure of opinion per single occurrence. The harmonic average of $m_{i,j}$, for all occurrences of j and over all users, provides an average community weighted rating of a single generalised occurrence in a or, more simply, the community socio-technical indicator β_j. This value can be used as a recommender system, so as to automatically compute hypothetical ratings for posts and, also, to alter user socio-technical indicators.

MANIPULATING THE USER SOCIO-TECHNICAL INDICATOR

User socio-technical indicators must not only be sensitive to changes in a user's processes or contributions, but must also be sensitive to evolution in community norms, in terms of both the quality and the quantity of attributes that they represent. With respect to quality, we are concerned with changes in both the direction and the magnitude of user indicators and community indicators. Direction indicates whether a community approves or disapproves of an attribute; Magnitude indicates the extent of the approval or disapproval. Since β_j represents the average rating for an attribute, the measure of the direction of an attribute can be extracted from it. Simply, the community can be said to approve of an attribute j if $\beta_j > 0$, or to disapprove of it if $\beta_j < 0$. If $\beta_j = 0$, however, then the ratings balance out and no clear consensus can be deduced from the community as to this regard. The value of β_j can be used to set a 'sign bit' which indicates the direction of the attribute. For the purpose of applicability to further formulae, the sign bit is represented as the scalar s, which can assume any of the values shown in Table 2. The extent of the direction of the community can also be determined from the community socio-technical indicator β_j, as it is simply the absolute value of β_j.

Table 2:

Sign Bit Values

Type	$\beta_j \neq 0$ (Consensus Deduced)		$\beta_j = 0$ (Consensus Not Deduced)
	$\beta_j < 0$	$\beta_j > 0$	$\beta_j = 0$
Range	$\beta_j < 0$	$\beta_j > 0$	$\beta_j = 0$
Scalars	$\beta_j / |\beta_j| = -1$	$\beta_j / |\beta_j| = 1$	$\beta_j = 0$

Since a user is an individual within the collective of the community, their contributions are valued with regards to the norms of the community. On a superficial level, this implies that a user's socio-technical indicator $\alpha_{i,j}$ must be related in some fashion to a user's mean weighted-rating $m_{i,j}$, to the community's generalised opinion β_j (both in terms of direction and magnitude). One formula for achieving this relationship is to alter $\alpha_{i,j}$ with regards to the ratio of a user's weighted-rating for each occurrence in a to the community's weighted-rating for each occurrence in a generalised a, or, more precisely, the scalar $f = (m_{i,j} / \beta_j)$. However, this formula considers only the value of the single generalised occurrence of an attribute, and it does not take into account the value of the entire contribution or process, which may consist of multiple occurrences. That is, the formula measures value whilst ignoring quantity. Thus, in measuring the value of an entire contribution, it is necessary to apply the value of the unitary occurrence to each occurrence within the contribution. In order to maintain a controlled system, this value can be included with respect to the community's average of occurrences, $\overline{a_j}$. Additionally, the direction of the attribute should be considered: If the community approves of the attribute, then the user's socio-technical indicator should be increase by f; alternatively, if the community disapproves of the attribute, then the user's socio-technical indicator should decrease by f. This provides us with the more appropriate value:

$$f = \frac{m_{i,j}}{\beta_j} \times \frac{a_{i,j}}{\overline{a_j}} \times s$$

The simplified recursive definition for manipulating user i's socio-technical indicator for an attribute j is $\alpha_{i,j[k+1]} = (f_{i,j} + \alpha_{i,j[k]})$, where k is simply an ordinal recurrence index. Since direction is multiplied into the formula, this allows us the intuitive option of simply summing all of the indicators of a user in order to calculate a representative user status. Negatively construed (i.e. where f<0) attributes will provide a decrease in status and positively construed attributes (i.e. where f>0) will provide an increase. If the community has not reached a consensus as to the value of the attribute, then the quantity which modifies the indicator equates to zero (e.g. f=0), and the user status is not changed. Given f, such a definition provides for four mutually-exclusive scenarios, presented in Table 3.

Table 3:

Exhaustive scenarios for causes and effects on user status

Scenario	$m_{i,j}$	β_j	$(m_{i,j} \div \beta_j)$	$f = \dfrac{m_{i,j}}{\beta_j} \times \dfrac{a_{i,j}}{a_j} \times s$	Effect on alpha
A	-	-	+	-	←
B	-	+	-	-	←
C	+	-	-	+	→
D	+	+	+	+	→

Perhaps, the outcomes in Table 3 are best understood through the adoption of two intuitively valued attributes, say 'profanity' and 'length of post'. For simplicity, in scenario A and C, where the community disapproves of the attribute, we shall consider that attribute to be 'profanity'. In scenarios B and D, where the community approves of the attribute, we shall consider that attribute to be 'length of post' – that is, the community approves of posts of an ideal length. In case A, the average rating for a contribution is negative and it can be inferred that the community does not approve of the post, with regards to profanity; hypothetically, the post might contain many occurrences of profanity and it has a negative rating in order to reflect this. The calculation of post quality (i.e. $m_{i,j}/\beta_j$) would result in a positive scalar as, at least on an analytic level, the user is conforming to community rating for profanity. Yet, since the norm for this attribute is one of disapproval, the sign bit reverses the rating to a negative scalar. Similarly, in case C, the community opinion is negative, but the user's post is rated positively. This is, given a negative rating in the quality calculation because the user's rating differs from that of the communities. Yet since the community's rating for the attribute is one of disapproval, the rating is reversed so as to have a positive effect on user status. Considering the attribute of 'post length', of which the community generally approves, a user who writes short messages receives a reduced status, such as in Scenario B. Conversely, a user who writes longer messages, such as in a Scenario D, receives a positive increment to their status. It should be noted that, although it is more intuitive to consider the table in terms of two attributes, it is equally valid and applicable in terms of a single attribute. For instance, Scenarios B and D could also represent a community which approves of profanity. The outcomes are verified by comparing the contribution rating $m_{i,j}$ with the effect on user i's status: user status should increase in contributions for which the community approves, and decrease in contributions for which the community disapproves. The attractiveness of the formula is that it is natural and intuitively appealing, whilst considering quality, in both direction and magnitude, and quantity.

DETECTING BIAS THROUGH A CONTEXT EFFECT

Further, the model is capable of identifying bias within the community. The quality ratio, $m_{i,j}/\beta_j$, makes differences between contribution ratings and general ratings explicit, for any single occurrence of a given attribute j. Through such a ratio, discrepancies between posts and community norms, or a *context effect*, can be easily identified. For instance, a user who is consistently rated poorly, due to a personal dislike of the user within the community, would consistently achieve lower ratings per attribute. Similarly, users who are personally preferred would consistently achieve higher ratings. Furthermore, the ratio can be used to measure the context effect of an attribute's degree. That is, although the scope of an attribute may be generalised, specific variations in the individual occurrences can be identified. For example, an occurrence of the attribute 'profanity' may be considered as being extremely offensive in one community, while the same occurrence may be considered as relatively insignificant in another. Hence, the Socio-Technical Indicator Model allows for the implementations of mechanisms to manage bias within a community.

Modelling Integrated Socio-technical Feedback Systems

Single Attribute Simulation

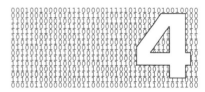

MONTE CARLO AND MATHEMATICAL EXPLORATIONS OF CONVERGENCE, STABILITY AND RELATIVE STATUS

The Socio-Technical Indicator Model does not guarantee convergence, neither for the user socio-technical indicators $\alpha_{i,j}$ or community socio-technical indicator β_j. The purpose of the Monte Carlo simulation that is now reported was to explore, within the application of representative moderation, issues of convergence for user and community indicators.

Monte Carlo simulation has distinct advantages over mathematical description for systems that model feedback using multi-layered embedded functions, such as the Socio-Technical Indicator Model – particularly substantial advantages in simplicity and efficiency for exploring multi-process social feedback models of competing valued attributes in democratic systems, which are a subset of possible representative moderations offered by Socio-Technical Indicator Model (Reed, & Clark, 2002).

It is reasonable to assume that, if convergence is demonstrated for single attributes of the model, this will imply convergence for systems described by profiles of multiple independent attributes. Hence, convergence was explored for a single attribute. The demonstration attribute was the negative valuing of profanity in a representatively moderated communications of a virtual community.

The convergence issues explored were:
1. Convergence for a single attribute of user status $\alpha_{i,j}$ and community health β_j

Given convergence, then:
2. How is the relative status of Special Interest Groups (SIGs) influenced by their proportions within the community?

This second issue is of particular importance in e-democracy applications where the SIGs are designated by different value sets corresponding to actual political issues.

ASCRIPTION OF PARAMETERS

The application now simulated is described in Chapter 3 and the parameters are as ascribed in Table 1: 'Parameters and Functions of an Application to Moderation'. The representatively moderated communications process is that individual SIG users post attribute-laden communications 'a_j'. These are then assessed, perhaps with bias, by other interested individual users according to their own SIG values '$r_{i,j}$'. Status, commensurate with each biased assessment, is awarded from each interested user to the individual originator of the post through 'Change in

Status' function '$f E_{i,j}$'. Originators of posts, and thus their SIGs, increase in status for the attribute. The cumulative status of SIG members shows the status of each SIG within the community and the total of all statuses shows the health of the community 'b_j' in terms of the attribute 'j'. In an e-democracy, application status would represent influence and could be assigned through representational options within the model including rounding dichotomously to represent various voting systems as described above in Chapter 3 'Calculating the Community Socio-Technical Indicator' page 38.

Special Interest Groups (SIGs)

The arbitrary attribute of value used in the single attribute simulation was the number of occurrences of 'profanity' within the posts of system users. This attribute was negatively valued by the community as a whole. Hence, the 'health' of the community was monitored through the mean profanities per post. Through this metric, the evolution of the health of the community, along a series of successive posting cycles, was analysed. Specifically, the health of the community decreased if the mean profanities per post increased, as this increase can be said to conflict with community values. Conversely, the health of the community can be considered to increase if the average profanities per post decreased with the successive posting cycle. However, SIGs would represent sub-groups of members with various values dissenting from the average value. Hence, SIGs could vary from consisting of minority members that valued profanity in posts, and so represented high dissent within the community, to SIGs consisting of more conservative members that who most value no profanity.

All parameters other than SIG group proportions were fixed for this initial exploration of convergence and SIG group influence. The fixed values were chosen to intuitively fit to the context of the application and parsimoniously generate sufficiently varied results to adequately inform the two issues. Hence, being in mind of the illustrious three body problem in Physics (for example, Barrow-Green, 1996; Szebehely, 1967; Valtonen, & Karttunen, forthcoming), only three SIG groups were set as a minimum number to hopefully generate a rich variety of informative outcomes with possible analogies between masses of the planets and proportions of the SIGs; specifically, these groups were High Profanity users, Average Profanity users and Low Profanity users (hereon referred to as the High SIG, the Average SIG and the Low SIG, respectively).

Generating SIG occurrences of the attribute

Occurrences of profanity within each post were generated using a standard multiplicative pseudo-random number generator, of which the seed was set by the computer clock. However, it was considered more realistic to generate the occurrences at random from a Normal distribution $N(m, s^2)$ as, in practice, such behaviour is mostly well described by this distribution. The mean occurrence of profanity in each post of each user, or m, reflected the SIG values of the users. Variations and skewness in the distributions of occurrences were modelled through fixing values of the variance s^2 and cut-off boundaries x_1 and x_2 to the distributions as in Table 4.

Table 4:

Fixed parameters determining
SIG distributions for attribute
occurrences

	Mean	Std	lower bound	upper bound
SIG	μ	σ	x_1	x_2
High	9	1	8	11
Average	1	2.5	1	8
Low	1	0	1	1

These distributions are illustrated in Figure 3.

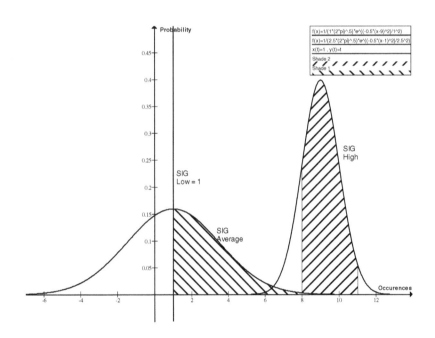

Figure 3: Probability distributions
generating SIG attribute
occurrences

Generating SIG value weightings of occurrences

It was considered reasonable to assume that SIG users would systematically assess a unit profanity according to some monotonic function, either increasing or decreasing to match their approval or disapproval. For simplicity, a pro-rata bias in accordance with their values was assumed. Hence, three linear functions were used to generate assessments of occurrences weighted according to the values of the SIGs, viz. High SIG users assessed high occurrences of profanity as high and low occurrences of profanity as low, Low SIG users assessed low occurrences of profanity as high and high occurrences of profanity as low, and Average SIG users would fall between the two other SIGs but closer to the Low SIG users who represented the initial values of the community. An additional 'noise' factor would be those assessors' idiosyncratic values which are independent of the attribute and arise due to interaction with non-attribute values represented in the content – both simulate idiosyncratic influence. This was subsumed in the variations of random normal occurrences. The three linear functions that were used are displayed in Table 5 where y is an assessment and x is an occurrence. The relative domains of these functions can be compared through the illustration in Figure 4.

Table 5:

Linear functions simulating SIG
members' pro-rata value
biased assessments of
occurrences

Assessment	Weighting y=a+bx	
SIG	a	b
High	-5	1
Average	3	0.5
Low	5	-1

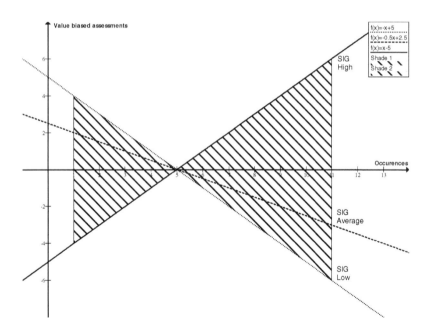

Figure 4: Relative domains of SIG members' value
biased assessments of occurrences

Number of users and their probabilities of posting and responding

The number of users, and the probabilities of users in each SIG group posting and replying, were set at N=300, 20%:60%:20% and 20%:30%:20% for High, Average and Low SIG members respectively. This was in consideration of the effects of the Law of Large Numbers and of convergence under the Central Limit Theorem on the discrimination of simulation techniques (Arsham, 1990, 1996) in conjunction with our available computing power – an Intel Pentium 4, 2.8ghz processor and 512mb Random Access Memory.

The probability of posting represented the 'interest' of a SIG member in communicating with the group by originating a post. Similarly, the probability of replying represented the interest of a SIG member in responding to any post. It was expected that these selection probabilities with 300 users would result in statistically acceptable 60 to 160 original postings and assessment replies to each post, a range of 3600 to 25600 assessment replies for each SIG in each cycle. For more efficient computation the same random occurrence was programmed for each member of the same SIG which, by the Central Limit Theorem, maintained a generous variation of response and which calculated through 20 feedback posting cycles was expected to significantly reduce processing time to an acceptable 5 minutes with our available computing power.

The program code is presented in Appendix 1.

SEQUENCING OF SIMULATIONS

As described in Section 4, convergence and the evolution of SIG status were to be investigated. This was achieved, in reverse order, by setting the parameters for three scenarios of SIG proportions A, B and C, and testing the convergence and stability of each set by running three simulations of each set. Each set was initialised to the same starting positions and each set was subjected to 20 posting cycles. Hence, nine simulations are presented, being three of set A, named A1, A2 and A3, followed by three of set B, named B1, B2 and B3, and finishing with three of set C, named C1, C2 and C3.

In order to assess convergence and stability, results *within* sets were compared. In order to assess the influence of SIG proportions on the relative status of the SIGs and on the 'health' of the community, results *between* sets were compared.

Table 6:

Sequencing of three stochastic
trials under each of three
proportionality conditions

TRIALS A1 to A3			TRIALS B1 to B3			TRIALS C1 to C3		
SIG	i	Proportions	SIG	i	Proportions	SIG	i	Proportions
High	1	20	High	1	10	High	1	10
Average	2	60	Average	2	70	Average	2	60
Low	3	20	Low	3	20	Low	3	30

Table 6 also shows the progression between the three proportionality conditions viz. after Trials A1 to A3, 10% of the High SIG members migrated to the Average SIG, and after Trials

B1 to B3, 10% of the Average SIG members migrated to the Low SIG. This migration of SIG membership towards the rewarded community values might be as expected in the virtual community.

EXPECTED RESULTS

As stated in Chapter 4, the Socio-Technical Indicator Model does not guarantee convergence. Since the model only processes positive feedback, it is entirely possible that a forced feedback loop could be created under some values of the parameters and that the system would collapse out of control. For example, one SIG could become increasingly dominant, and through increasingly promoting themselves without competition, would destroy the community by meaninglessly exponentially increasing their status to infinity. Alternatively, other initial states could produce immediate or delayed chaos, or successive stages of chaos and recovery. Our scientific zeitgeist would suggest the last option.

Assuming that simulated input to the feedback functions did result in convergence, then the relative status of the groups, sans feedback, would be predicted by the assessments given to mean occurrences of the SIGs under each of the three conditions of proportionality. These mean occurrences can be estimated from the shaded distributions illustrated in Figure 3 and calculated from the corresponding parameters listed in Table 4.

Calculations of expected mean occurrences for each SIG

The Normal distribution function was used to calculate the expected value of occurrences for each SIG as follows:

The mean value of occurrences between x_1 and x_2 under $N(\mu,\sigma^2)$ is m' where:

$$\Phi(m)= \tfrac{1}{2}(P_1<x_1 - P_2<x_2) + (P_1<x_1), \; \forall \; (x_1, x_{2)} \in N(\mu,\sigma^2)$$

Simply, `m' is the ordinate between x_1 and x_2 that cuts the area in half.

For the SIG High $x_1= 8$, $x_2 = 11$, $\mu= 9$, $\sigma=1$

$\therefore \Phi(m_h) = 0.909297307$

$\quad m_h = 10.336440348$

For the SIG Average $x_1= 1$, $x_2 = 8$, $\mu=1$, $\sigma=2.5$

$\therefore \Phi(m_a) = 0.748722435$

$\quad m_a = 2.676187138$

For the SIG Low

$\quad m= 1$

Expected relative status for each SIG under three proportionality conditions

When the effect of representation feedback is excluded, status will be determined by the mean occurrences produced by each SIG, weighted by their value biased assessment, multiplied by the SIG proportions and simply totalled. The model, it must be remembered, excludes self-assessment. This would be similar to prohibiting voting for oneself. Table 7 presents these fixed calculations for each SIG under each of the three proportionality conditions A, B and C.

Table 7:

Non-Stochastic expectations
of relative SIG status under
three proportionality
conditions

Expected status and ranking of thee SIGs
Without feedback   Note - Self-assessments are excluded

A TRIAL		Proportions	Mean Occurrence	Mean assessments from		
				High	Average	Low
SIG	i		a_i	f_{a1}	f_{a2}	f_{a3}
High	1	20	10.34	-	-2.67	-5.34
Average	2	60	2.68	-2.32	-	2.32
Low	3	20	1.00	-4.00	2.00	-

A TRIAL		Proportions	Total Assessments	Expected Status	Ranked Highest
SIG	i		f_B		
High	1	20	-8.00	-160.1	3
Average	2	60	0.00	0.0	1
Low	3	20	-2.00	-40.0	2

B TRIAL		Proportions	Mean Occurrence	Mean assessments from		
				High	Average	Low
SIG	i		a_i	f_{a1}	f_{a2}	f_{a3}
High	1	10	10.34	-	-2.67	-5.34
Average	2	70	2.68	-2.32	-	2.32
Low	3	20	1.00	-4.00	2.00	-

B TRIAL		Proportions	Total Assessments	Expected Status	Ranked Highest
SIG	i		f_B		
High	1	10	-8.00	-80.0	3
Average	2	70	0.00	0.0	1
Low	3	20	-2.00	-40.0	2

C TRIAL		Proportions	Mean Occurrence	Mean assessments from		
				High	Average	Low
SIG	i		a_i	f_{a1}	f_{a2}	f_{a3}
High	1	10	10.34	-	-2.67	-5.34
Average	2	60	2.68	-2.32	-	2.32
Low	3	30	1.00	-4.00	2.00	-

C TRIAL		Proportions	Total Assessments	Expected Status	Ranked Highest
SIG	i		f_B		
High	1	10	-8.00	-80.0	3
Average	2	60	0.00	0.0	1
Low	3	30	-2.00	-60.0	2

It might be intuitively expected in a community that disfavours profanity that Low profanity users (mean $=1$) would have a higher status than Average profanity users (mean$=2.68$) and that the Highest profanity users would have the lowest status. However, whereas the expected result is that the Highest profanity users do seem to attain the lowest status, there is a non-intuitive reverse in the fortunes of the Average and Low profanity users. The Average profanity users are expected to attain the highest status when stochastic feedback is excluded.

The symmetries in Figure 4 lead may partially explain this expectation and also suggest an expected zero-sum mirroring of the High and Low SIGs. The functions representing the High and Low SIG values can be seen from Figure 4 to be mirrors of one another. This implies that what every status is awarded to one group in any post cycle will be at the expense of the other, and so the status trends of the two SIGs can be expected to substantially mirror each other during stable posting cycles.

Figure 5 shows the same biased assessments of the SIGs as in Figure 4, except that the X-Y central symmetrical section has been 'blocked out'. It is this section that contributes equitable to the status of both the High and Low SIGs. What is left exposed on the right of the diagram are the domains that represent the assessment of occurrences in the range 9 to 11.

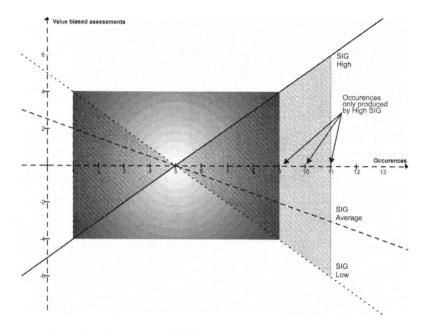

Figure 5: Symmetries of SIG members'
value biased assessments

It is seen from Figure 3 that these levels of profanity, in the range 9 to 11, are exclusively produced by the High SIG. The High SIG – Low SIG X symmetry in this range continues to ensure the mirroring of status by the two groups. However, these high occurrences of profanity from the High SIG are unsymmetrical penalised by the conservative values of the Average SIG members. In addition, the Average SIG membership also awards status for low occurrences of profanity in the range 1 to 5. Figure 3 shows that only the Low SIG members and Average SIG members themselves produce occurrences in this range, and because self-assessment is prohibited by the model, occurrences in this range can only contribute to the status of the Low SIG. Hence, the effect of the Average SIG asymmetry disadvantages the High SIG in the 9 to 11 range and advantages the Low SIG for single occurrences. All else is equal between the High and Low SIGs. Hence, the High SIGs can be expected to attain the lowest status as is also shown by the expectation all three proportionality conditions in Table 6.

Secondary analyses of SIG status and community health

It was possible that similarity in the status of the SIGs with the most differing values, the High SIG and the Low SIG, could be reflected in the overall health of the community. Hence, secondary analyses of the output were used to explore associative trend patterns between changes in the health of the community and changes in the differences of status between the High and Low SIG members. The differences between mean Low SIG status and mean High SIG status were calculated at each post cycle. First order differences in these changes were matched with first order differences in mean community health at each post cycle. Matching changes showing either that successive mean values were closer or more distant, were flagged with '-' and '+' respectively, and the percentages of matched pairs were calculated for both first and second order differences. It was expected that these percentages might indicate differences in convergent and non-convergent results and differences between convergent and non-convergent stable outcomes.

EMPERICAL RESULTS

The code presented in Appendix 1 was run nine times under sequenced conditions A1 to C3 as described in Section 4.2 'Sequencing of simulations' and summarised in Table 7. The output is presented in Appendix 2 and described in this section.

TRIALS A1 TO A3 UNDER HIGH, AVERAGE AND LOW SIG PROPORTIONS OF 20%, 60% AND 20%

Trial A1 with SIG proportions of 20%, 60% and 20%

Table 8:

Trial A1 with High, Average
and Low SIG proportions of
20%, 60% and 20%

TRIAL A 1

Post#	beta	High	Av	Low	High+Low
1	0.17	-14.63	0.25	-85.61	-100.24
2	0.26	-30.95	-10.78	-58.25	-89.20
3	0.37	-36.00	-12.27	-51.71	-87.71
4	0.48	-37.31	-12.93	-49.75	-87.06
5	0.5	-37.99	-13.28	-48.72	-86.71
6	0.47	-37.98	-13.47	-48.54	-86.52
7	0.55	-38.84	-13.65	-47.50	-86.34
8	0.54	-38.62	-13.73	-47.63	-86.25
9	0.67	-39.53	-13.75	-46.70	-86.23
10	0.6	-39.66	-13.69	-46.64	-86.30
11	0.56	-39.39	-13.68	-46.91	-86.30
12	-0.88	-40.75	-13.72	-45.51	-86.26
13	-0.49	-39.21	-13.68	-47.10	-86.31
14	-1.35	-41.59	-13.70	-44.69	-86.28
15	-2.75	-42.35	-13.70	-43.93	-86.28
16	-1.66	-41.83	-13.66	-44.49	-86.32
17	-3.08	-42.37	-13.64	-43.97	-86.34
18	-6.29	-42.74	-13.64	-43.61	-86.35
19	-6.29	-42.71	-13.64	-43.64	-86.35
20	-6.81	-42.72	-13.63	-43.63	-86.35

Figure 6:   Trial A1 with High, Average and Low SIG proportions
of 20%, 60% and 20%

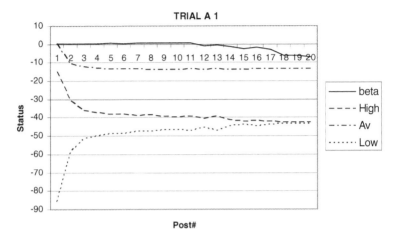

Table 9:

Trial A1 trend analyses of SIG
status differences and
community health

Secondary analyses

TRIAL A 1		1st order Differences						2nd order Differences				
Post#	beta	Low-High	beta	Low-High	beta	High-Low	m	beta	Low-High	beta	Low-High	m
1	0.17	-70.98										
2	0.26	-27.30	0.09	43.68	+	+	1					
3	0.37	-15.71	0.11	11.59	+	+	1	0.02	-32.09	-	-	1
4	0.48	-12.44	0.11	3.27	+	+	1	0.00	-8.32	-	-	1
5	0.5	-10.73	0.02	1.71	+	+	1	-0.09	-1.56	-	-	1
6	0.47	-10.56	-0.03	0.17	-	+		-0.05	-1.54	-	-	1
7	0.55	-8.66	0.08	1.90	+	+	1	0.11	1.73	+	-	
8	0.54	-9.01	-0.01	-0.35	-	-	1	-0.09	-2.25	-	-	1
9	0.67	-7.17	0.13	1.84	+	+	1	0.14	2.19	+	+	1
10	0.6	-6.98	-0.07	0.19	-	+		-0.20	-1.65	-	-	1
11	0.56	-7.52	-0.04	-0.54	-	-	1	0.03	-0.73	-	-	1
12	-0.88	-4.76	-1.44	2.76	-	+		-1.40	3.30	-	+	
13	-0.49	-7.89	0.39	-3.13	+	-		1.83	-5.89	+	-	
14	-1.35	-3.10	-0.86	4.79	-	+		-1.25	7.92	-	+	
15	-2.75	-1.58	-1.40	1.52	-	+		-0.54	-3.27	-	-	1
16	-1.66	-2.66	1.09	-1.08	+	-		2.49	-2.60	+	-	
17	-3.08	-1.60	-1.42	1.06	-	+		-2.51	2.14	-	+	
18	-6.29	-0.87	-3.21	0.73	-	+		-1.79	-0.33	-	-	1
19	-6.29	-0.93	0.00	-0.06	-	-	1	3.21	-0.79	-	-	1
20	-6.81	-0.91	-0.52	0.02	-	+		-0.52	0.08	-	+	
				% Matches	47					% Matches	61	

Convergence: Results for Trial A1 showed initial rapid convergence over posts #1 to #3 to stable status of High and Low SIGs towards the same value of -43 by post #18.

Stability: The Average SIG status stabilised even more rapidly to -13 due to much less variation in the status of the SIG. At post #12 the gap between High SIG and Low SIG status had narrowed from 70.98 at post #1 to 4.76. At the same post cycle the health of the community, beta, which had remained stable and just positive dipped from 0.56 into the negative at -0.88. Beta eventually stabilises at -6.8.

Relative SIG status: The expected mirrored trends of the High and Low SIG status resulted as expected. However the ranked status of these two SIGs was reversed from the expected priority of 2,3 to 3,2. This difference in rank was of little consequence as both SIGs eventually converge to the same stable value of -43. Interestingly, after post #6, the Average SIG maintained a very small variation in its status between -13.67 and -13.73.

Secondary analyses: There was a sudden jump in the Low-High status 1st order differences of 2.76 at p0st #18 that corresponded to the dip in community health from positive to negative. Matches in trend changes were low at 47% for 1st order differences, and these were mainly for posts #1 to #11, not at the convergent range of the posting cycles.

Trial A2 with SIG proportions of 20%, 60% and 20%

Table 10:

Trial A2 with High, Average
and Low SIG proportions of
20%, 60% and 20%

TRIAL A 2

Post#	beta	High	Av	Low	High+Low
1	0.16	-18.11	-7.08	-74.80	-92.91
2	0.40	-32.95	-11.35	-55.68	-88.63
3	0.56	-35.38	-12.29	-52.31	-87.69
4	0.55	-36.28	-12.74	-50.97	-87.25
5	0.81	-38.74	-12.86	-48.39	-87.13
6	0.74	-38.32	-12.95	-48.72	-87.04
7	0.44	-36.39	-12.94	-50.66	-87.05
8	1.17	-40.46	-13.07	-46.46	-86.92
9	0.38	-35.96	-13.00	-51.03	-86.99
10	-0.09	-30.00	-12.86	-57.12	-87.12
11	-2.93	-42.74	-13.18	-44.07	-86.81
12	-9.63	-43.12	-13.18	-43.68	-86.80
13	-12.04	-43.13	-13.18	-43.67	-86.80
14	-16.70	-43.18	-13.18	-43.63	-86.81
15	-21.14	-43.20	-13.18	-43.60	-86.80
16	-28.30	-43.23	-13.18	-43.57	-86.80
17	-32.89	-43.24	-13.18	-43.56	-86.80
18	-36.25	-43.25	-13.18	-43.56	-86.81
19	-38.88	-43.25	-13.18	-43.55	-86.80
20	-44.90	-43.26	-13.18	-43.54	-86.80

Figure 7: Trial A2 with High, Average and Low SIG proportions of 20%, 60% and 20%

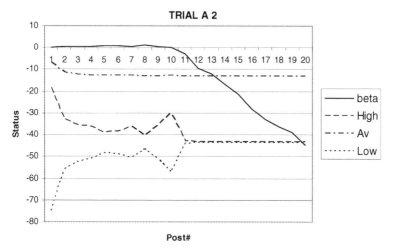

Table 11:

Trial A2 trend analyses of SIG
status differences and
community health

Secondary analyses

TRIAL A 2			1st order Differences					2nd order Differences				
Post#	beta	Low-High	beta	Low-High	beta	High-Low	m	beta	Low-High	beta	Low-High	m
1	0.16	-56.69										
2	0.4	-22.73	0.24	33.96	+	+	1					
3	0.56	-16.93	0.16	5.80	+	+	1	-0.08	-28.16	-	-	1
4	0.55	-14.69	-0.01	2.24	-	+		-0.17	-3.56	-	-	1
5	0.81	-9.65	0.26	5.04	+	+	1	0.27	2.80	+	-	
6	0.74	-10.40	-0.07	-0.75	-	-	1	-0.33	-5.79	-	-	1
7	0.44	-14.27	-0.30	-3.87	-	-	1	-0.23	-3.12	-	-	1
8	1.17	-6.00	0.73	8.27	+	+	1	1.03	12.14	+	+	1
9	0.38	-15.07	-0.79	-9.07	-	-	1	-1.52	-17.34	-	-	1
10	-0.09	-27.12	-0.47	-12.05	-	-	1	0.32	-2.98	-	-	1
11	-2.93	-1.33	-2.84	25.79	-	+		-2.37	37.84	-	+	
12	-9.63	-0.56	-6.70	0.77	-	+		-3.86	-25.02	-	-	1
13	-12	-0.54	-2.41	0.02	-	+		4.29	-0.75	-	-	1
14	-16.7	-0.45	-4.66	0.09	-	+		-2.25	0.07	-	-	1
15	-21.1	-0.40	-4.44	0.05	-	+		0.22	-0.04	-	-	1
16	-28.3	-0.34	-7.16	0.06	-	+		-2.72	0.01	-	-	1
17	-32.9	-0.32	-4.59	0.02	-	+		2.57	-0.04	-	-	1
18	-36.3	-0.31	-3.36	0.01	-	+		1.23	-0.01	-	-	1
19	-38.9	-0.30	-2.63	0.01	-	+		0.73	0.00	-	-	1
20	-44.9	-0.28	-6.02	0.02	-	+		-3.39	0.01	-	-	1
					% Matches		42			% Matches		89

Convergence: The results for trial A2 converged more rapidly and suddenly for the HIGH and LOW SIGs than trial A1 which used the same initial conditions. The convergence occurred from the post #10 to post #11 from a difference of 27.12 to a difference of only 1.33.

Stability: The status of the High and Low SIGs became stable at essentially the same value of -43 by post #12. The Average SIG again became stable earlier by post #4 at -12.7. It remained very stable at -13.18 for 10 post cycles from post #11 to the end of the trial. It was most noticeable that the health of the community became unstable when the High and Low SIGs attained equal status. The community health continued to plummet rapidly through the end of the trial. The detrimental effect on community health, concurrent with a small difference in the SIG status between the two SIGs with the most differing values, was noticed in trail A1 and seems to be confirmed by trial A2.

Relative SIG status: The expected mirrored trends of the High and Low SIG status resulted as expected. However the ranked status of these two SIGs was again reversed from the expected priority of 2,3 to 3,2. This difference in rank was again of little consequence as both SIGs eventually converge to the same stable value of -43 as they did in trial A1. The Average SIG maintained it position with top status as expected.

Secondary analyses: There was a jump in the Low-High 1st order to 25.76 difference at post #11 which corresponded with corresponded with the collapse of community health. The matches were low for matches in 1st order differences at 42%, all of which occurred before the collapse in community health. Matches in 2nd order differences were high at 89%.

Trial A3 with SIG proportions of 20%, 60% and 20%

Table 12:

Trial A3 with High, Average and Low SIG proportions of 20%, 60% and 20%

TRIAL A 3

Post#	beta	High	Av	Low	High+Low
1	0.18	-14.22	-1.55	-84.22	-98.44
2	0.32	-34.06	-10.13	-55.79	-89.85
3	0.44	-37.01	-11.75	-51.22	-88.23
4	0.53	-37.59	-12.31	-50.08	-87.67
5	0.64	-38.99	-12.59	-48.41	-87.40
6	0.74	-39.80	-12.78	-47.40	-87.20
7	0.79	-40.34	-12.84	-46.81	-87.15
8	1.02	-40.83	-12.93	-46.23	-87.06
9	0.78	-40.11	-13.10	-46.77	-86.88
10	1.16	-41.01	-13.20	-45.78	-86.79
11	0.87	-40.56	-13.21	-46.22	-86.78
12	1.14	-41.34	-13.22	-45.42	-86.76
13	0.97	-41.04	-13.19	-45.76	-86.80
14	0.55	-39.72	-13.11	-47.15	-86.87
15	0.69	-40.54	-13.13	-46.31	-86.85
16	1.31	-41.80	-13.17	-45.01	-86.81
17	1.49	-41.99	-13.17	-44.82	-86.81
18	2.02	-42.33	-13.16	-44.50	-86.83
19	1.39	-41.78	-13.13	-45.07	-86.85
20	0.29	-37.68	-13.08	-49.23	-86.91

Figure 8: Trial A3 with High, Average and Low SIG proportions
of 20%, 60% and 20%

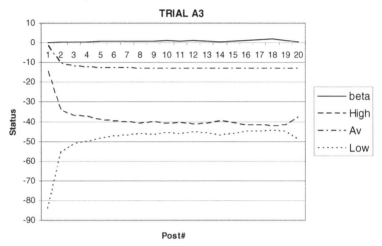

Table 13:

Trial A3 trend analyses of SIG
status differences and
community health

Secondary analyses

TRIAL A 3			1st order Differences					2nd order Differences				
Post#	beta	Low-High	beta	Low-High	beta	High-Low	m	beta	Low-High	beta	Low-High	m
1	0.18	-70.00										
2	0.32	-21.73	0.14	48.27	+	+	1					
3	0.44	-14.21	0.12	7.52	+	+	1	-0.02	-40.75	-	-	1
4	0.53	-12.49	0.09	1.72	+	+	1	-0.03	-5.80	-	-	1
5	0.64	-9.42	0.11	3.07	+	+	1	0.02	1.35	-	-	1
6	0.74	-7.60	0.10	1.82	+	+	1	-0.01	-1.25	-	-	1
7	0.79	-6.47	0.05	1.13	+	+	1	-0.05	-0.69	-	-	1
8	1.02	-5.40	0.23	1.07	+	+	1	0.18	-0.06	-	-	1
9	0.78	-6.66	-0.24	-1.26	-	-	1	-0.47	-2.33	-	-	1
10	1.16	-4.77	0.38	1.89	+	+	1	0.62	3.15	+	+	1
11	0.87	-5.66	-0.29	-0.89	-	-	1	-0.67	-2.78	-	-	1
12	1.14	-4.08	0.27	1.58	+	+	1	0.56	2.47	+	+	1
13	0.97	-4.72	-0.17	-0.64	-	-	1	-0.44	-2.22	-	-	1
14	0.55	-7.43	-0.42	-2.71	-	-	1	-0.25	-2.07	-	-	1
15	0.69	-5.77	0.14	1.66	+	+	1	0.56	4.37	+	+	1
16	1.31	-3.21	0.62	2.56	+	+	1	0.48	0.90	-	-	1
17	1.49	-2.83	0.18	0.38	+	+	1	-0.44	-2.18	-	-	1
18	2.02	-2.17	0.53	0.66	+	+	1	0.35	0.28	-	-	1
19	1.39	-3.29	-0.63	-1.12	-	-	1	-1.16	-1.78	-	-	1
20	0.29	-11.55	-1.10	-8.26	-	-	1	-0.47	-7.14	-	-	1
			% Matches		100				% Matches		100	

Convergence: The mirrored status trends of the High and Low SIGs slowly converged to between -42 and -44, their closest being 2.17 at post #18. Then they separated to a distance of 11.55 at post #20.

Stability: Community health stayed just positive and stable over all 20 posts.

Relative SIG status: The relative status ranking of the three SIGs remained as in trials A1 and A2 with the Average SIG attaining the highest status as expected and maintaining it at -13, as was the case in the trials A1 and A2.

Secondary analyses: This was a very interesting result with 100% matches between 1st order differences in changes in High and Low SIG status and changes in community health.

This seemed to be a stable healthy system result up to the end of the posting cycle at post #20.

Trials B1 to B3 under High, Average and Low SIG Proportions of 10%, 70% and 20%

For these three trials, 10% of the High SIG members migrated into the Average SIG

Trial B1 with SIG proportions of 10%, 70% and 20%

Table 14:

Trial B1 with High, Average
and Low SIG proportions of
10%, 70% and 20%

TRIAL B 1

Post#	beta	High	Av	Low	High+Low
1	0.33	7.59	140.61	-48.20	-40.61
2	0.40	-75.18	29.41	-54.22	-129.40
3	0.48	-68.97	12.43	-43.46	-112.43
4	0.55	-66.09	6.88	-40.79	-106.88
5	0.63	-65.45	4.55	-39.10	-104.55
6	0.68	-65.12	3.38	-38.26	-103.38
7	0.75	-64.72	2.61	-37.89	-102.61
8	0.82	-64.69	2.12	-37.42	-102.11
9	0.89	-64.59	1.74	-37.14	-101.73
10	0.93	-65.05	1.52	-36.47	-101.52
11	0.96	-64.89	1.33	-36.44	-101.33
12	1.04	-64.68	1.02	-36.33	-101.01
13	1.09	-64.73	0.74	-36.00	-100.73
14	1.08	-65.04	0.64	-35.60	-100.64
15	1.19	-65.25	0.54	-35.29	-100.54
16	1.15	-65.46	0.52	-35.05	-100.51
17	1.19	-65.48	0.42	-34.93	-100.41
18	1.28	-65.71	0.35	-34.64	-100.35
19	1.32	-66.01	0.38	-34.36	-100.37
20	1.29	-66.18	0.47	-34.28	-100.46

Figure 9: Trial B1 with High, Average and Low SIG proportions of 10%, 70% and 20%

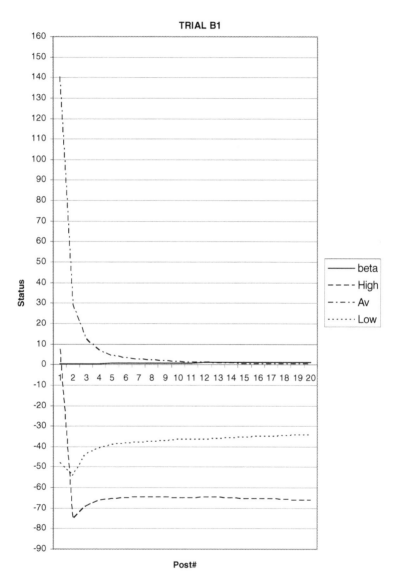

Table 15:

Trial B1 trend analyses of SIG
status differences and
community health

Secondary analyses

TRIAL B 1			1st order Differences					2nd order Differences				
Post#	beta	Low-High	beta	Low-High	beta	High-Low	m	beta	Low-High	beta	Low-High	m
1	0.33	-55.79										
2	0.4	20.96	0.07	76.75	+	+	1					
3	0.48	25.51	0.08	4.55	+	+	1	0.01	-72.20	-	-	1
4	0.55	25.30	0.07	-0.21	+	-		-0.01	-4.76	-	-	1
5	0.63	26.35	0.08	1.05	+	+	1	0.01	1.26	-	+	
6	0.68	26.86	0.05	0.51	+	+	1	-0.03	-0.54	-	-	1
7	0.75	26.83	0.07	-0.03	+	-		0.02	-0.54	-	-	1
8	0.82	27.27	0.07	0.44	+	+	1	0.00	0.47	-	+	
9	0.89	27.45	0.07	0.18	+	+	1	0.00	-0.26	-	-	1
10	0.93	28.58	0.04	1.13	+	+	1	-0.03	0.95	-	-	1
11	0.96	28.45	0.03	-0.13	+	-		-0.01	-1.26	-	-	1
12	1.04	28.35	0.08	-0.10	+	-		0.05	0.03	-	-	1
13	1.09	28.73	0.05	0.38	+	+	1	-0.03	0.48	-	+	
14	1.08	29.44	-0.01	0.71	-	+		-0.06	0.33	-	-	1
15	1.19	29.96	0.11	0.52	+	+	1	0.12	-0.19	+	-	
16	1.15	30.41	-0.04	0.45	-	+		-0.15	-0.07	-	-	1
17	1.19	30.55	0.04	0.14	+	+	1	0.08	-0.31	+	-	
18	1.28	31.07	0.09	0.52	+	+	1	0.05	0.38	-	-	1
19	1.32	31.65	0.04	0.58	+	+	1	-0.05	0.06	-	-	1
20	1.29	31.90	-0.03	0.25	-	+		-0.07	-0.33	-	-	1
					% Matches		63			% Matches		72

Convergence: The system converged quickly, by post #3.

Stability: Stability was achieved with convergence at post #3
even though results of the first post were highly varied. Beta
stayed positive, reaching a high of 1.32 at post #18.

Relative SIG status: The relative order of the High and Low SIG
status changed on the second post giving the expected status
ranking of Average SIG, Low SIG and High SIG. The mirror trend
result was broken for the first time over the first few posts of
this cycle.

Secondary analyses: The High and Low SIGs maintained a slightly increasing difference over posts #4 to #20. The 62% 1st order differences matches were evenly spread over the 20 post cycle.

Trial B2 with SIG proportions of 10%, 70% and 20%

Table 16:

Trial B2 with High, Average
and Low SIG proportions of
10%, 70% and 20%

TRIAL B2

Post#	beta	High	Av	Low	High+Low
1	0.19	-45.22	14.06	-68.84	-114.06
2	0.28	-57.40	-2.70	-39.89	-97.29
3	0.40	-61.78	-4.16	-34.05	-95.83
4	0.50	-62.49	-4.81	-32.69	-95.18
5	0.53	-62.11	-5.28	-32.59	-94.70
6	0.65	-62.92	-5.51	-31.55	-94.47
7	0.72	-63.38	-5.65	-30.96	-94.34
8	0.83	-63.59	-5.77	-30.62	-94.21
9	0.95	-64.26	-5.80	-29.93	-94.19
10	0.84	-64.21	-5.82	-29.95	-94.16
11	0.91	-64.42	-5.83	-29.73	-94.15
12	1.06	-64.33	-5.88	-29.77	-94.10
13	1.04	-63.93	-5.98	-30.07	-94.00
14	1.05	-63.88	-6.09	-30.01	-93.89
15	1.26	-64.13	-6.17	-29.69	-93.82
16	1.34	-64.21	-6.21	-29.56	-93.77
17	1.15	-64.08	-6.23	-29.67	-93.75
18	1.33	-64.44	-6.21	-29.34	-93.78
19	0.55	-62.93	-6.24	-30.81	-93.74
20	1.05	-64.30	-6.21	-29.48	-93.78

Figure 10: Trial B2 with High, Average and Low SIG proportions of 10%, 70% and 20%

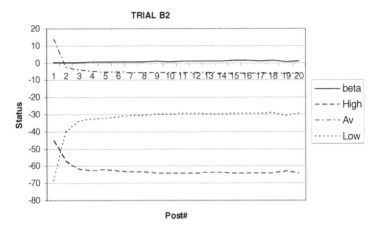

Table 17:

Trial B2 trend analyses of SIG
status differences and
community health

Secondary analyses

TRIAL B2			1st order Differences					2nd order Differences				
Post#	beta	Low-High	beta	Low-High	beta	High-Low	m	beta	Low-High	beta	Low-High	m
1	0.19	-23.62										
2	0.28	17.51	0.09	41.13	+	+	1					
3	0.4	27.73	0.12	10.22	+	+	1	0.03	-30.91	-	-	1
4	0.5	29.80	0.10	2.07	+	+	1	-0.02	-8.15	-	-	1
5	0.53	29.52	0.03	-0.28	+	-		-0.07	-2.35	-	-	1
6	0.65	31.37	0.12	1.85	+	+	1	0.09	2.13	-	+	
7	0.72	32.42	0.07	1.05	+	+	1	-0.05	-0.80	-	-	1
8	0.83	32.97	0.11	0.55	+	+	1	0.04	-0.50	-	-	1
9	0.95	34.33	0.12	1.36	+	+	1	0.01	0.81	-	-	1
10	0.84	34.26	-0.11	-0.07	-	-	1	-0.23	-1.43	-	-	1
11	0.91	34.69	0.07	0.43	+	+	1	0.18	0.50	+	+	1
12	1.06	34.56	0.15	-0.13	+	-		0.08	-0.56	-	-	1
13	1.04	33.86	-0.02	-0.70	-	-	1	-0.17	-0.57	-	-	1
14	1.05	33.87	0.01	0.01	+	+	1	0.03	0.71	+	+	1
15	1.26	34.44	0.21	0.57	+	+	1	0.20	0.56	-	-	1
16	1.34	34.65	0.08	0.21	+	+	1	-0.13	-0.36	-	-	1
17	1.15	34.41	-0.19	-0.24	-	-	1	-0.27	-0.45	-	-	1
18	1.33	35.10	0.18	0.69	+	+	1	0.37	0.93	+	+	1
19	0.55	32.12	-0.78	-2.98	-	-	1	-0.96	-3.67	-	-	1
20	1.05	34.82	0.50	2.70	+	+	1	1.28	5.68	+	+	1
				% Matches		89				% Matches		94

Convergence: Although post #1 results were not so extreme as for trial B1, this trail converged similarly to B1.

Stability: The system became stable by post #6 with the High SIG status between -63 and -65, and the Low SIG status between -31 and -29. The status of the Average SIG slowly stabilised to around -6.2 over the complete 20-post cycle

Relative SIG status: After a variable start, the relative status positions of the High and Low SIGs quickly stabilised into the expected order. The beta stayed positive at around one.

Secondary analyses: There were high percentage matches for both the 1st order difference trends at 89%, and for the 2nd order difference trends at 94%. The large stable difference of 33 that was maintained between the status of the High and Low SIGs appeared to contribute to a healthy stable system.

Trial B3 with SIG proportions of 10%, 70% and 20%

Table 18:

Trial B3 with High, Average
and Low SIG proportions of
10%, 70% and 20%

TRIAL B3

Post#	beta	High	Av	Low	High+Low
1	0.22	-40.86	3.47	-62.61	-103.47
2	0.36	-55.49	-4.10	-40.40	-95.89
3	0.47	-57.94	-5.45	-36.59	-94.53
4	0.62	-59.01	-5.90	-35.07	-94.08
5	0.69	-59.14	-6.24	-34.60	-93.74
6	0.86	-60.08	-6.44	-33.47	-93.55
7	0.97	-60.43	-6.56	-33.00	-93.43
8	1.00	-60.80	-6.63	-32.56	-93.36
9	1.37	-61.54	-6.65	-31.80	-93.34
10	1.60	-61.89	-6.63	-31.46	-93.35
11	1.81	-62.07	-6.63	-31.29	-93.36
12	1.90	-62.28	-6.60	-31.11	-93.39
13	1.80	-62.35	-6.55	-31.08	-93.43
14	0.97	-61.39	-6.51	-32.08	-93.47
15	1.72	-62.88	-6.43	-30.67	-93.55
16	2.24	-63.21	-6.39	-30.38	-93.59
17	1.49	-62.61	-6.38	-30.99	-93.60
18	1.08	-62.15	-6.36	-31.47	-93.62
19	0.00	-40.62	-6.61	-52.75	-93.37
20	-57.91	-64.39	-6.26	-29.33	-93.72

Figure 11: Trial B3 with High, Average and Low SIG proportions of 10%, 70% and 20%

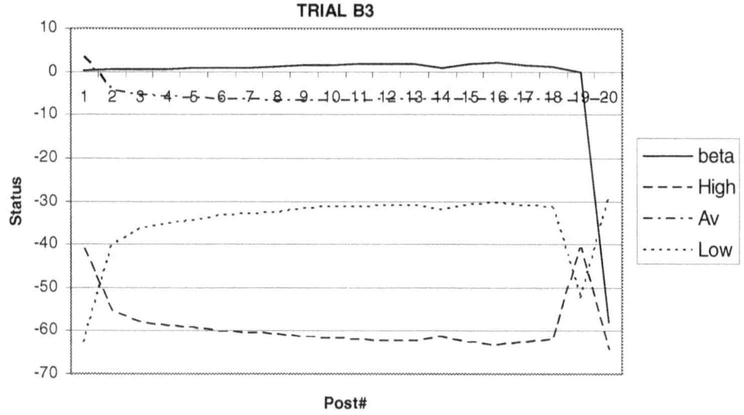

Table 19:

Trial B3 trend analyses of SIG status differences and community health

Secondary analyses

TRIAL B3			1st order Differences					2nd order Differences				
Post#	beta	Low-High	beta	Low-High	beta	High-Low	m	beta	Low-High	beta	Low-High	m
1	0.22	-21.75										
2	0.36	15.09	0.14	36.84	+	+	1					
3	0.47	21.35	0.11	6.26	+	+	1	-0.03	-30.58	-	-	1
4	0.62	23.94	0.15	2.59	+	+	1	0.04	-3.67	-	-	1
5	0.69	24.54	0.07	0.60	+	+	1	-0.08	-1.99	-	-	1
6	0.86	26.61	0.17	2.07	+	+	1	0.10	1.47	-	-	1
7	0.97	27.43	0.11	0.82	+	+	1	-0.06	-1.25	-	-	1
8	1	28.24	0.03	0.81	+	+	1	-0.08	-0.01	-	-	1
9	1.37	29.74	0.37	1.50	+	+	1	0.34	0.69	-	-	1
10	1.6	30.43	0.23	0.69	+	+	1	-0.14	-0.81	-	-	1
11	1.81	30.78	0.21	0.35	+	+	1	-0.02	-0.34	-	-	1
12	1.9	31.17	0.09	0.39	+	+	1	-0.12	0.04	-	-	1
13	1.8	31.27	-0.10	0.10	-	+		-0.19	-0.29	-	-	1
14	0.97	29.31	-0.83	-1.96	-	-	1	-0.73	-2.06	-	-	1
15	1.72	32.21	0.75	2.90	+	+	1	1.58	4.86	+	+	1
16	2.24	32.83	0.52	0.62	+	+	1	-0.23	-2.28	-	-	1
17	1.49	31.62	-0.75	-1.21	-	-	1	-1.27	-1.83	-	-	1
18	1.08	30.68	-0.41	-0.94	-	-	1	0.34	0.27	-	-	1
19	0	-12.13	-1.08	-42.81	-	-	1	-0.67	-41.87	-	-	1
20	-57.9	35.06	-57.91	47.19	-	+		-56.83	90.00	-	+	
					% Matches		89			% Matches		94

Convergence: This is a most interesting result. The system quickly converges by post #4, then a catastrophic change hit the system at post #19.

Stability: The status of the Average SIG remained stable, but this did not prevent the system from collapsing as the High and Low SIGs suddenly changed status. This seems to indicate that the stability of the system is more dependent on the extreme SIGs than on the average SIG.

Relative SIG status: After a variable start the order of SIG status quickly returns to the expected order of Average, Low and High, and remains like this until the change over during the system collapse at post #19.

Secondary analyses: The 2nd order differences show that the system converged and temporarily stabilised at post #4 with a 2nd order High-Low difference of -30.58 to -3,67. This leaped from 0.27 to -41.87 at post #19. However, this only reflects the actual status changes rather than predicting them. There was , however a large perturbation anomaly from -2.06 to 4.86 in the 2nd order differences at post #15 that might have predicted the sudden changes in SIG status affecting the High and Low SIGs. This was perhaps 'foreshadowed' by the smaller 1st order perturbation at post #12 when the betas reached a local maximum.

TRIALS C1 TO B3 UNDER HIGH, AVERAGE AND LOW SIG PROPORTIONS OF 10%, 60% AND 30%

For this sequence 10% of the Average SIG membership migrated to the Low SIG.

Trial C1 with proportions of 10%, 60% and 30%

Table 20:

Trial C1 with High, Average and Low SIG proportions of 10%, 60% and 30%

TRIAL C1

Post#	beta	High	Av	Low	High+Low
1	0.29	-58.85	8.12	-49.27	-108.12
2	0.42	-65.62	-5.81	-28.56	-94.18
3	0.52	-65.89	-7.59	-26.50	-92.39
4	0.66	-67.69	-7.85	-24.45	-92.14
5	0.63	-66.75	-8.30	-24.94	-91.69
6	0.74	-66.53	-8.68	-24.77	-91.30
7	0.84	-66.78	-8.87	-24.33	-91.11
8	0.90	-66.61	-9.08	-24.30	-90.91
9	0.93	-66.95	-9.11	-23.93	-90.88
10	0.92	-66.88	-9.12	-23.99	-90.87
11	1.12	-67.13	-9.15	-23.70	-90.83
12	1.38	-67.58	-9.15	-23.25	-90.83
13	0.93	-66.67	-9.33	-23.98	-90.65
14	1.31	-67.69	-9.26	-23.04	-90.73
15	1.16	-67.52	-9.30	-23.16	-90.68
16	1.62	-68.26	-9.23	-22.50	-90.76
17	0.76	-67.04	-9.34	-23.60	-90.64
18	1.29	-68.14	-9.23	-22.62	-90.76
19	1.46	-68.40	-9.17	-22.41	-90.81
20	2.10	-68.74	-9.13	-22.11	-90.85

Figure 12: Trial C1 with High, Average and Low SIG proportions
of 10%, 60% and 30%

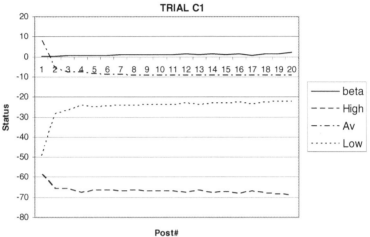

Table 21:

Trial C1 trend analyses of SIG
status differences and
community health

Secondary analyses

TRIAL C1			1st order Differences					2nd order Differences				
Post#	beta	Low-High	beta	Low-High	beta	High-Low	m	beta	Low-High	beta	Low-High	m
1	0.29	9.58										
2	0.42	37.06	0.13	27.48	+	+	1					
3	0.52	39.39	0.10	2.33	+	+	1	-0.03	-25.15	-	-	1
4	0.66	43.24	0.14	3.85	+	+	1	0.04	1.52	-	-	1
5	0.63	41.81	-0.03	-1.43	-	-	1	-0.17	-5.28	-	-	1
6	0.74	41.76	0.11	-0.05	+	-		0.14	1.38	+	-	
7	0.84	42.45	0.10	0.69	+	+	1	-0.01	0.74	-	+	
8	0.9	42.31	0.06	-0.14	+	-		-0.04	-0.83	-	-	1
9	0.93	43.02	0.03	0.71	+	+	1	-0.03	0.85	-	+	
10	0.92	42.89	-0.01	-0.13	-	-	1	-0.04	-0.84	-	-	1
11	1.12	43.43	0.20	0.54	+	+	1	0.21	0.67	+	+	1
12	1.38	44.33	0.26	0.90	+	+	1	0.06	0.36	-	-	1
13	0.93	42.69	-0.45	-1.64	-	-	1	-0.71	-2.54	-	-	1
14	1.31	44.65	0.38	1.96	+	+	1	0.83	3.60	+	+	1
15	1.16	44.36	-0.15	-0.29	-	-	1	-0.53	-2.25	-	-	1
16	1.62	45.76	0.46	1.40	+	+	1	0.61	1.69	+	+	1
17	0.76	43.44	-0.86	-2.32	-	-	1	-1.32	-3.72	-	-	1
18	1.29	45.52	0.53	2.08	+	+	1	1.39	4.40	+	+	1
19	1.46	45.99	0.17	0.47	+	+	1	-0.36	-1.61	-	-	1
20	2.1	46.63	0.64	0.64	+	+	1	0.47	0.17	-	-	1
			% Matches		89				% Matches		83	

Convergence: The system converges very slowly over the 20-post cycle.

Stability: The status trend of the Average SIG seems to asymptote to -9. The High and Low SIG status moved slowly towards -69 and -22 respectively over the 20-post cycle.

Relative SIG status: The last four posts resulted in an increasing separation of the High and Low SIGs and this was accompanied by a rise to the highest beta over all trials to this point.

Secondary analyses: There were high percentages of 1st and 2nd order difference matches of 89% and 83% respectively, both with 100% matches in the last half of the cycle – posts #10 to #20.

Trial C2 with proportions of 10%, 60% and 30%

Table 22:

Trial C2 with High, Average
and Low SIG proportions of
10%, 60% and 30%

TRIAL C2

Post#	beta	High	Av	Low	High+Low
1	0.30	-90.51	37.51	-46.99	-137.50
2	0.47	-72.44	-1.88	-25.66	-98.10
3	0.64	-76.55	-3.29	-20.14	-96.69
4	0.83	-76.21	-3.62	-20.15	-96.36
5	0.84	-75.23	-4.31	-20.45	-95.68
6	1.08	-75.42	-4.66	-19.90	-95.32
7	1.07	-74.49	-5.17	-20.32	-94.81
8	1.22	-74.42	-5.54	-20.03	-94.45
9	1.36	-74.14	-5.82	-20.02	-94.16
10	1.52	-73.97	-6.06	-19.95	-93.92
11	1.36	-73.77	-6.21	-20.00	-93.77
12	1.62	-74.04	-6.25	-19.70	-93.74
13	1.93	-73.99	-6.33	-19.67	-93.66
14	1.92	-73.95	-6.38	-19.65	-93.60
15	2.10	-73.89	-6.44	-19.66	-93.55
16	1.94	-73.73	-6.49	-19.76	-93.49
17	2.37	-73.87	-6.52	-19.59	-93.46
18	1.90	-73.68	-6.55	-19.76	-93.44
19	2.04	-73.76	-6.54	-19.69	-93.45
20	1.98	-73.56	-6.58	-19.84	-93.40

Figure 13: Trial C2 with High, Average and Low SIG proportions of 10%, 60% and 30%

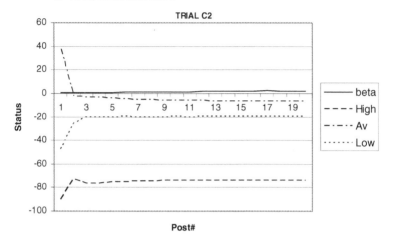

Table 23:

Trial C2 trend analyses of SIG
status differences and
community health

Secondary analyses

TRIAL C2			1st order Differences					2nd order Differences				
Post#	beta	Low-High	beta	Low-High	beta	High-Low	m	beta	Low-High	beta	Low-High	m
1	0.3	43.52										
2	0.47	46.78	0.17	3.26	+	+	1					
3	0.64	56.41	0.17	9.63	+	+	1	0.00	6.37	-	-	1
4	0.83	56.06	0.19	-0.35	+	-		0.02	-9.98	-	-	1
5	0.84	54.78	0.01	-1.28	+	-		-0.18	-0.93	-	-	1
6	1.08	55.52	0.24	0.74	+	+	1	0.23	2.02	-	+	
7	1.07	54.17	-0.01	-1.35	-	-	1	-0.25	-2.09	-	-	1
8	1.22	54.39	0.15	0.22	+	+	1	0.16	1.57	+	+	1
9	1.36	54.12	0.14	-0.27	+	-		-0.01	-0.49	-	-	1
10	1.52	54.02	0.16	-0.10	+	-		0.02	0.17	-	-	1
11	1.36	53.77	-0.16	-0.25	-	-	1	-0.32	-0.15	-	-	1
12	1.62	54.34	0.26	0.57	+	+	1	0.42	0.82	+	+	1
13	1.93	54.32	0.31	-0.02	+	-		0.05	-0.59	-	-	1
14	1.92	54.30	-0.01	-0.02	-	-	1	-0.32	0.00	-	-	1
15	2.1	54.23	0.18	-0.07	+	-		0.19	-0.05	+	-	
16	1.94	53.97	-0.16	-0.26	-	-	1	-0.34	-0.19	-	-	1
17	2.37	54.28	0.43	0.31	+	+	1	0.59	0.57	+	+	1
18	1.9	53.92	-0.47	-0.36	-	-	1	-0.90	-0.67	-	-	1
19	2.04	54.07	0.14	0.15	+	+	1	0.61	0.51	+	+	1
20	1.98	53.72	-0.06	-0.35	-	-	1	-0.20	-0.50	-	-	1
					% Matches	68				% Matches		89

Convergence: The system quickly converges at post #4.

Stability: A healthy sign was that the mean betas reach a high of 2.37 at post #17 and stabilised. All SIG groups quickly attained and maintained a stable status.

Relative SIG status: Similarly to trial B1, the mirror status trends of the High and Low SIGs were broken over the first few posts of this cycle and seem to have been mirrored between the Low SIG and the Average SIG. The status ranking started as expected and this was maintained.

Secondary analyses: A large High-Low difference in SIG status between 53 and 54 was attained quickly by post #7 and maintained through the cycle.

Trial C3 with proportions of 10%, 60% and 30%

Table 24:

Trial C3 with High, Average
and Low SIG proportions of
10%, 60% and 30%

TRIAL C3

Post#	beta	High	Av	Low	High+Low
1	0.35	-69.73	14.41	-44.68	-114.41
2	0.53	-71.46	-3.70	-24.83	-96.29
3	0.68	-69.74	-6.24	-24.01	-93.75
4	0.87	-70.22	-7.06	-22.71	-92.93
5	1.12	-71.53	-7.22	-21.24	-92.77
6	1.16	-71.39	-7.42	-21.18	-92.57
7	1.24	-71.53	-7.56	-20.90	-92.43
8	1.33	-71.52	-7.66	-20.80	-92.32
9	1.27	-71.71	-7.71	-20.56	-92.27
10	1.27	-71.63	-7.79	-20.57	-92.20
11	1.15	-71.40	-7.87	-20.71	-92.11
12	1.04	-71.25	-7.96	-20.78	-92.03
13	1.24	-71.63	-7.95	-20.40	-92.03
14	1.92	-72.26	-7.89	-19.84	-92.10
15	2.39	-72.42	-7.87	-19.69	-92.11
16	2.29	-72.34	-7.89	-19.76	-92.10
17	1.27	-71.37	-8.03	-20.59	-91.96
18	0.74	-70.21	-8.20	-21.58	-91.79
19	0.96	-71.10	-8.09	-20.79	-91.89
20	-0.73	-70.62	-8.16	-21.21	-91.83

Figure 14: Trial C3 with High, Average and Low SIG proportions
of 10%, 60% and 30%

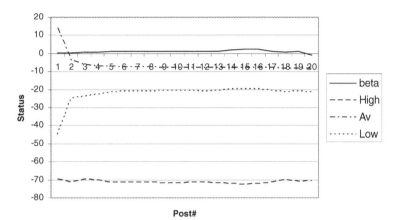

TRAIL C3

Table 25:

Trial C3 trend analyses of SIG
status differences and
community health

Secondary analyses

TRIAL C3			1st order Differences					2nd order Differences				
Post#	beta	Low-High	beta	Low-High	beta	High-Low	m	beta	Low-High	beta	Low-High	m
1	0.35	25.05										
2	0.53	46.63	0.18	21.58	+	+	1					
3	0.68	45.73	0.15	-0.90	+	-		-0.03	-22.48	-	-	1
4	0.87	47.51	0.19	1.78	+	+	1	0.04	2.68	-	+	
5	1.12	50.29	0.25	2.78	+	+	1	0.06	1.00	-	-	1
6	1.16	50.21	0.04	-0.08	+	-		-0.21	-2.86	-	-	1
7	1.24	50.63	0.08	0.42	+	+	1	0.04	0.50	-	+	
8	1.33	50.72	0.09	0.09	+	+	1	0.01	-0.33	-	-	1
9	1.27	51.15	-0.06	0.43	-	+		-0.15	0.34	-	-	1
10	1.27	51.06	0.00	-0.09	-	-	1	0.06	-0.52	-	-	1
11	1.15	50.69	-0.12	-0.37	-	-	1	-0.12	-0.28	-	-	1
12	1.04	50.47	-0.11	-0.22	-	-	1	0.01	0.15	-	-	1
13	1.24	51.23	0.20	0.76	+	+	1	0.31	0.98	+	+	1
14	1.92	52.42	0.68	1.19	+	+	1	0.48	0.43	-	-	1
15	2.39	52.73	0.47	0.31	+	+	1	-0.21	-0.88	-	-	1
16	2.29	52.58	-0.10	-0.15	-	-	1	-0.57	-0.46	-	-	1
17	1.27	50.78	-1.02	-1.80	-	-	1	-0.92	-1.65	-	-	1
18	0.74	48.63	-0.53	-2.15	-	-	1	0.49	-0.35	-	-	1
19	0.96	50.31	0.22	1.68	+	+	1	0.75	3.83	+	+	1
20	-0.73	49.41	-1.69	-0.90	-	-	1	-1.91	-2.58	-	-	1
				% Matches		84				% Matches		89

Convergence: The system converged quickly by the 4th post.

Stability: This mean betas remained stable and the highest of all trials reaching a global maximum of 2.37 at post #15.

Relative SIG status: Similarly to B1 and C2, the High-Low mirror-trends seemed not to apply over the first few posts but were evident between the Low and Average SIGs during the first three posts.

Secondary analyses: 1st and 2nd order difference matches were very high at 84% and 89% respectively; with 100% 1st and 2nd order difference matches over the last 10 posts.

DISCUSSION

This simulation explored the convergence and stability of the model for one attribute for three SIGs, a High value SIG an Average value SIG and Low value SIG, under three different proportions of SIG membership. The community norm was to be in favour of low value. The proportions started at condition 'A' of 20:60:20 and three trials were run A1, A2 and A3. For the second condition, 10% of the High SIG membership migrated to the Average SIG to give proportions of 10:70:20. Three trials were run under this condition; B1, B2 and B3. Finally, 10% of the Average SIG membership migrated to the Low SIG giving the proportions of 10:60:30, and three trials were run with these values, C1, C2 and C3.

Results showed that the model exhibited convergence under all three conditions. However, the model also showed that the system becomes unstable when the extreme value SIGs attain near equal status. This condition is likely to be inhibited in conditions, like trial C, where the contrary value SIG is in a smaller proportion.

Influences on community health

The initial trial A1 showed that when the statuses of High and Low value SIGs converge then community health drops. This suggested the need for a minimum diversity of values to maintain a healthy community. This effect was strongly confirmed in trial A2 when the status of High and Low SIGs converged early and the community health plummeted. From this result it could be inferred that a difference in status between SIGs with extreme values is necessary for maintaining the health of the community. Trial A3 supported this by showing that maintaining the stable status of SIGs with the most differing values maintained community health.

Related influences on stability and convergence: self-recovery of collapsed systems

Trial B3 seemed to support the assumption that a system will remain healthy (positive betas) when a stable difference in status is maintained between the High and Low SIG members. For example, C1 showed the mean betas climbed to high of 2.10 at post #20 while the status of the High and Low SIGs was still gradually diverging. However, trial B3 was a surprise. The status of the Average SIG remained stable, but this did not prevent the system from collapsing. This seems to indicate that the stability of the system is more dependent on the extreme SIGs than the on the Average SIG, particularly as this set of trials contained the largest percentage, 70%, in the average SIG. Why did it collapse and would it have recovered given a longer post cycle? In trial A3 the status of High and Low SIGs converged at post #18 and then diverged. This indicated that the simulation needs to be re-run with more cycles to ascertain if convergence continues or if change becomes chaotic, and if it does become chaotic whether the system can recover. Although trial A3 showed a healthy community result, the similar status of the High and Low SIGs might have indicated imminent destabilisation.

It is unlikely that simulations with longer post-cycles will show that collapsed systems are capable of self-recovery. It is not a varied status of the SIGs that would prevent a system self-recovery, because some trials converged from highly varied positions at post #1. What might hamper or prevent self-recovery is the low beta health of the system that accompanies the collapse. This implies that a chaotic system with highly diverse status positions could be stabilised from that situation by positive external influences on the system health. Realistically, it might be more practical for the collapsed system's community to migrate, with their differing values, to an extant healthy functioning system. This option favours several small supportive community systems, ready to host migrant membership, rather than one encompassing system. However, this recommendation fits what could be only one of many forms of system collapse. The proportions of the C trials gave the highest sustained community health and maintained large stable status differences between the High and Low SIGs. Trial B2 showed that high percentage matching of 1st and 2nd order differences over the last 10 posts, as in the cases of trials B2, C1, C2, C3 and notably A3, is not an infallible indicator of stability.

Summary

It seems that a divergence of values is necessary for the continued good health and stability of representational moderated system. However, the group with values most contrary to the standards of the community needs to be in the smallest proportion. In addition, when the Average value group is in the majority, this seemed to result in the highest sustained health of the whole community.

Modelling Integrated Socio-technical Feedback Systems

Extended Applications

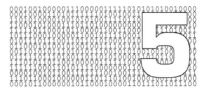

The Socio-Technical Indicator Model lends itself to multiple extended applications, two of which are detailed in Table 26 on the next page. A brief discussion of each application is provided below.

MODELLING BIO-CONSERVATION SYSTEMS

In application to bio-conservation, the modelling is populated by species, with each species producing and/or consuming resources that affect their population. For any single resource, j, each species, $i...n,$ produces a given amount of the resource, or $a_{i,j}$. For instance, if that resource is honey, bees might produce some quantity of honey ($a_{i,j} > 0$), while bears may not produce any ($a_{i,j} = 0$). Other species may have use for that resource, as bears may consume bees' honey, and the quantity of a resource that each member of a particular species uses is represented by $r_{i,j}$. The total amount of a resource that a species will consume is proportionate to both the size of the species (i.e. $\alpha_{i,j}$) and the

Table 26:

Parameters and Functions of Two Extended Applications

Model		Marketing model		Bio-conservation model	
		Descriptor	Formulea	Descriptor	Formulea
System parameters	i	Merchant	-	Species (e.g. woodpecker, snake, squirel)	-
	j	Atribute of a product	-	Resource related to population growth/decrease	-
Internal parameters	α_i	Wealth of merchant i	-	Population size of species i	-
	a	Number of occurences of an attribute within a product	-	Amount of Resource j produced by specieces	-
	$r_{i,j}$	Value of product j to user i	-	Individual requirement of species i's members for resource j	Preset constant
Functions	$f_{Ai,j}$	Amount i is willing to pay because of this property	$\dfrac{\alpha}{\sqrt{2\pi}} \int_{-\infty}^{r} e^{-\frac{r^2}{2}} dr$	Amount of a_{ij} consumed (by a single species external to i)	αr
	$f_{Bi,j}$	Value of aij from coistomers of merchant i, exposed to aij	$\sum_{i=1\ldots i-1}^{i+1\ldots n} \alpha_{i,j} r_{i,j}$	Amount of a_{ij} consumend by all species external to i	$\sum_{i=1\ldots i-1}^{i+1\ldots n} \alpha_{i,j} r_{i,j}$
	$f_{Ci,j}$	Value of unit attribute based on customers of merchant-exposed users	$\dfrac{f_{Bi,j}}{a_{i,j}}$	Amount of i's a_{ij} production left for the provider i	$a_{i,j} - f_{Ci,j}$
	$f_{Di,j}$	Average indirect market value of attribute	$\underset{i=1\ldots i-1}{\overset{i+1\ldots n}{HM}} (f_{Ci,j})$	Resource j available to all species (when $f_D >= 0$)	$\sum_{i=1}^{n} f_{Ci,j}$
	$f_{Ei,j}$	Total profit of a to merchant i	$a_{i,j}(f_D + f_C - C)$	Total production perceived as being avalable for species i	$\dfrac{f_D + f_C}{r}$

need of individuals within the species for a resource (i.e. $r_{i,j}$), or $fA=\alpha r$. The total amount of a resource consumed by all other species, or the sum of all fA for species, is fB. The amount of $a_{i,j}$ that remains after it has been partially or entirely consumed by members of other species is represented by fC. The amount of resources that remains in the environment, across the production of all species, is represented by a scalar fD, or the sum of all remaining resources. A negative scalar indicates that there exists a larger need for resources than there are resources available, whereas a positive scalar signifies that there exists more resource than there is need for that resource. The amount of a resource that the species produces in the future is viewed in relation to the amount of that resource available in their direct and indirect environment and to their need for that resource. The amount of self-produced resources that remain, or fC, being within the immediate environment of the individual, would also impact their future production. Additionally, the model can accommodate an awareness constant, which indicates how aware each species is of other species within its environment that consume that resource.

MODELLING PRODUCT MARKETS

Within the context of a financial application, the model provides for alterations in the wealth of merchants in a competitive market. A merchant *i* produces a product with an attribute *j*, such as size or weight. Other merchants in the market value the product, and this value is combined with their wealth in order to provide a scalar indicating an amount that each merchant is willing to spend on the product in order to purchase it. This scalar, fA can reasonably be considered a sigmoid function. In terms of the Socio-Technical Indicator Meta Model, the combination of these values, for each merchant, provides the *direct* market value of the product, that is, the total wealth that could be provided by the direct customers of merchant i's product. The ratio of total wealth to the number of occurrences, or, provides the direct value of each occurrence. The *indirect* market value of the product is provided through the harmonic mean of all values, exclusive of the direct market value for merchant i. Hence, the profit of merchant i, within the context of attribute j, is the cost of production (i.e. C) subtracted from the total value of all the occurrences of an attribute - that is the sum of the direct and indirect value of the product, multiplied by the number of occurrences of the attribute.

Conclusion

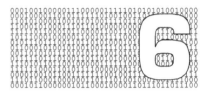

SOCIO-TECHNICAL INDICATOR MODEL

A Socio-Technical Indicator Model has been presented that operationalises, for multiple community-specific attributes, socio-technical indicators of characteristics that are valued by the community and that are responsive to the user collective. User responsiveness and monitoring of community values, is achieved through the community socio-technical indicators and individual user socio-technical indicators being derived as functions of basic parameters of on-going typical community communication processes. The basic parameters that have been identified can be chosen to represent fundamental characteristics of integrated feedback systems, and functions of those parameters can be flexibly chosen to simulate interactive processes that modify the community socio-technical indicators that monitor on-going valued states of these systems. Thus the model can simply describe a variety of complex, integrated feedback systems with multiple attributes and with structures as varied as bio-diversity, financial, and virtual community systems.

SELF-REGULATING REPRESENTATIVE E-SYSTEMS, AND OTHER APPLICATIONS

An illustrative application of the model has been detailed – one that can provide for on-line communities with evolving and self-regulating moderation mechanisms. The introduction of such mechanisms allows for the development of more representative systems than those implemented in current computer-mediated communication technologies. Indeed, computer-mediated communication technologies, have typically evolved in a cross-dichotomous manner, such that technical constructs of the technology have evolved independently from the social environment of the communities they serve. Hence, technical mechanisms of virtual community, such as moderation, have generally not been directly impacted by the community processes they moderate and, instead, have depended upon the external agency of community members to sensitize their operation within the static socio-technical environment of the community. Attempts to influence moderation by externally sensitizing the technology, as well as attempts to increase the representativeness of moderation, have been shown to restrict the flexibility of the community by inhibiting its evolution. In contrast, this detailed application of the model uniquely provides technical definitions of community values and attitudes, and allows for users to collectively monitor and control their communities in ways that promote the emergence of these values and attitudes.

The Socio-Technical Indicator Model simulates emergent valued characteristics of integrated multi-attributed communities. An illustrative application detailed here allows for more sensitive, representative and flexible systems of moderation for virtual communities such as e-democracies.

Modelling Integrated Socio-technical Feedback Systems

References

Arsham H. (1990). What-if Analysis in Computer Simulation Models: A Comparative Survey with Some Extensions, *Mathematical and Computer Modelling, 13*(1), 101-106.

Arsham H. (1996). Performance Extrapolation in Discrete-event Systems Simulation, *Journal of Systems Science, 27*(9), 863-869.

Barrow-Green, J. (1996). *Poincare and the Three Body Problem*. Providence, RI.: American Mathematical Society

Barry P.,Dekel U., Moraveji N., Weisz J. (2004). Increasing contribution in online communities using alternative displays of community activity levels. CHI 2004, April 24-29, 2004.

Berners-Lee, T. (1996). The World Wide Web: Past, Present and Future. Retrieved March 23rd, 2005 from: http://www.w3.org/People/Berners-Lee/1996/ppf.html

Berners-Lee, T. (n/d). The World Wide Web: A very short personal history. Retrieved March 23rd, 2005 from: http://www.w3.org/People/Berners-Lee/ShortHistory

Berners-Lee, T., Cailliau, R. (n/d). WorldWideWeb: Proposal for a HyperText Project. Retrieved March 23rd, 2005 from: http://www.w3.org/Proposal.html

Blanchard, A. L. and Markus, M. L. (2002). Sense of virtual community - Maintaining the experience of belonging. Proceedings of the 35th Hawaii International Conference on System Sciences, IEEE Computer Society, Volume 8.

Cain, B. E. (n/d). The Internet in the (Dis)Service of Democracy? Retrieved March 23rd, 2005 from: http://llr.lls.edu/volumes/v34-issue3/cain.pdf

Cosley, D., Frankowski, D., Kiesler, S., Terveen, L., Riedl, J. and CommunityLab (2005). How oversight improves member maintained communities. Proceedings of the ACM Conference on Human Factors in Computing Systems, CHI 2005, Portland, OR.

Coffman, K. G., Odlyzko (2000). Internet growth: Is there a "Moore's Law" for data traffic?. Retrieved March 23rd, 2005, from: http://www.dtc.umn.edu/~odlyzko/doc/internet.moore.pdf

Dahlberg, L. (2001a). Extending the Public Sphere through Cyberspace: The Case of Minnesota E-Democracy. *First Monday, 6*(3).

Dahlberg, L. (2001b). Computer-Mediated Communication and The Public Sphere: A Critical Analysis. *Journal of Computer-Mediated Communication, 7*(1).

Donath, J. S. (1998): Identity and deception in the virtual community. In Kollock, P. and Smith, M. (eds.). Communities in Cyberspace, London: Routledge.

Dreazen, Y. J. (2002). Wildly Optimistic Data Drove Telecoms to Build Fiber Glut. WALL ST. Journal, Sept. 26, 2002.

Farrand, Max (1937). The Records of the Federal Convention of 1787. Rev. ed. Vol. 2. New Haven and London: Yale University Press.

Follman, J. M. (2001). Getting the Web: Understanding the Nature and Meaning of the Internet. Chicargo, IL: Duomo Press.

Gillespie, B. (2001). IKS & the Information Society - synergism and antagonism. Presented at the International Conference on Indigenous Knowledge Systems. University of Venda for Science and Technology.

Golder, S. A. (2003). A Typology of Social Roles in Usenet. A thesis submitted to the Department of Linguistics, Harvard University.

Greening, D. R. (1989). Experiences With Cooperative Moderation of a Usenet Newsgroup. Proceedings of the 1989 ACM/IEEE Workshop on Applied Computing.

Hauben, M., Hauben, R. (1997). Netizens. Los Alaitos, CA: IEEE Computer Society Press.

Hauben, R. 2000. From ARPANET to Usenet News: On the Nourishment of the Net Commonwealth. Retrieved March 23rd, 2005, from: http://neil.franklin.ch/Netizen/ch.4_Arpa2Usenet

Joinson A. N. (2001). Self-disclosure in computer-mediated communication: The role of self-awareness and visual anonymity. European Journal of Social Psychology. Volume 31, Issue 2. Wiley, pp.177-192.

Kelly, S. U., Sung, C., & Farnham, S. (2002). Designing for Improved Social Responsibility, User Participation and Content in On-Line Communities. CHI Volume 1, Issue 1. ACM Press: New York.

Kollock, P., Smith, M. (1996). Managing the Virtual Commons: Cooperation and Conflict in Computer Communities Pp. 109-128 in Herring, S. (ed.). Computer-Mediated Communication: Linguistic, Social, and Cross-Cultural Perspectives. Amsterdam: John Benjamins.

Lampe, C., Resnick, P. (2004). Slash(dot) and Burn: Distributed Moderation in a Large Online Conversation Space. Proceedings of ACM Computer Human Interaction Conference, Vienna Austria.

Landfield, K. (2001). NetNews Moderator's Handbook. Retrieved March 23rd, 2005, from: http://www.landfield.com/usenet/moderators/handbook/

Li, H. (2004). Virtual Community Studies: A Literature Review, Synthesis and Research Agenda. Proceedings of the Americas Conference on Information Systems, New York, New York, August 2004, pp. 2608-2715.

Ludford, P.J., Cosley, D., Frankowski, D., & Terveen, L. (2004). Think Different: Increasing Online Community Participation Using Uniqueness and Group Dissimilarity. In *Proceedings of CHI 2004*, Vienna, Austria, pp. 631-638.

Mabry, E. (1996). Frames and Flames: The structure of argumentative messages on the 'net. In Sudweeks, F., McLaughlin, M. and Rafaeli, S. (eds). Network and Netplay: Virtual Groups on the Internet. Cambridge, MA: AAAI/MIT Press.

Margherio, L., Henry, D., Cooke, S. Montes, S., et al. (1998). The Emerging Digital Economy. Retrieved March 23rd, 2005 from: https://www.esa.doc.gov/Reports/EmergingDig.pdf

McKenna, K.Y. A and Bargh, J. (2000). Plan 9 from Cyberspace: The implications of the Internet for personality and social psychology. Personality and Social Psychology Review, 4, 57-75.

Netherlands National Commission for UNESCO (2005). Conference on Internet, Human Rights and Culture: Recommendations. Retrieved March 23rd, 2005 from: http://www.unesco.nl/images/recommendations.pdf

Nonnecke, B., Preece, J. (2000). Persistence and Lurkers in Discussion Lists: A Pilot Study. Retrieved May 29th, 2005, from: http://csdl.computer.org/comp/proceedings/hicss/2000/0493/03/04933031.pdf

Odlyzko, A. M. (2003). Internet traffic growth: Sources and implications. In Dingel, B. B., Weiershausen, W., Dutta, A. K., Sato, K. (eds.). Optical Transmission Systems and Equipment for WDM Networking II, Proc. SPIE, vol. 5247, 2003, pp. 1-15

Papadakis, M. C. (2003). Computer-Mediated Communities: The Implications of Information, Communication, and Computational Technologies for Creating Community Online. SRI International.

phpBB (n/d). phpBB 2.0 Full Guide. Retrieved March 27th, 2005, from: www.uscgaparents.org/phpBB2/fullguide.pdf

Rasmussen, T. (2003). On Distributed Society: The History of the Internet as a Guide to a Sociological Understanding of Communication and Society. In Liestøl G., Morrison A, & Rasmussen T. Digital Media Revisited The MIT Press.

Rinaldi, A.H. (1998). The Net: User Guidelines and Netiquette. Retrieved March 23rd, 2005 from: http://www.fau.edu/netiquette/net/.

Riva, G. (2001). Communicating in CMC: Making Order Out of Miscommunication. In Anolli, L., Ciceri, R. and Riva, G. (Eds.) Say not to Say: New perspectives on miscommunication. IOS Press.

Sansom, G. (1995). Illegal and Offensive Content on the Information Highway. Spectrum, Information Technologies and Telecommunications Sector (SITT), Industry Canada, June 19, 1995.

Spears, R and Lea, M. (1994). Panacea or panopticon? The hidden power in computer-mediated communication. Communication Research, 21, 427-459.

Szebehely, V. G. (1967). Theory of Orbits: *The Restricted Problem of Three Bodies*. New York: Academic Press.

Tehan, R. (2002). Internet Statistics: Explanation and Sources. Retrieved March 23rd, 2005 from: http://bubo.brynmawr.edu/~gtowell/rl31270.pdf

Templeton, B. (n/d). Reaction to the DEC Spam of 1978. Retrieved March 23rd, 2005, from: http://www.templetons.com/brad/spamreact.html

Valtonen, M., & Karttunen, K. (forthcoming, January 2006). *The Three-Body Problem*. Cambridge University Press.

Whittaker, S., L. Terveen, W. Hill, & L. Cherny (1998): The Dynamics of Mass Interaction. In CSCW 98, Seattle, Washington, USA. ACM, pp. 257-264.

Zakon, R. (1997). Request for Comments: 2235 (RFC2235). Network Working Group.

APPENDIX 1

Simulation Source Code

```
1 /*
2  * Main.java
3  *
4  * Zacharyas Boufoy-Bastick
5  * August 02, 2005
6  * This is a simulation of three groups within a community:
7  * high profanity users, average profanity users, and no profanity users
8  * their size, scope, and contribution probabilities are editable in-code
9
10 * Order of classes:
11 *
12 * Main
13 *  |
14 *  |— User
15 *  |— Contribution
16 *  |— Rating
17 */
18
19 import java.util.*;
20 import java.io.*;
21
22
23 public class Main {
24   //user data
25   public final static int USER_TOTAL = 300;      //number of users to
                                   generate
26   public final static int USER_HIGH_PROFANITY = 10;   //percentage of high
                                   profanity users
27   public final static int USER_NO_PROFANITY = 30;     //percentage of no
                                   profanity users
```

```
28   //interaction data
29   public final static int CONTRIBUTION_PROB_HIGH_PROFANITY = 20;   // %
                   probability of a high profanity user posting
30   public final static int CONTRIBUTION_PROB_AVERAGE_PROFANITY = 60; //
                   % probability of a avrg profanity user posting
31   public final static int CONTRIBUTION_PROB_NO_PROFANITY = 20;    // %
                   probability of a no profanity user posting
32   //profanity actual occurrence probability distribution
33   public final static int NO_PROFANITY_OCCURENCE = 1; //lowest profanity
                   occurrences value
34   public final static float  AVERAGE_PROFANITY_STANDARD_DEVIATION =
                   (float)2.5;
35   public final static float  AVERAGE_PROFANITY_MEAN = 4;
36   public final static double AVERAGE_PROFANITY_MIN = 1;
37   public final static double AVERAGE_PROFANITY_MAX = 7.9;
38   public final static float  HIGH_PROFANITY_STANDARD_DEVIATION =
                   (float)1.0;
39   public final static float  HIGH_PROFANITY_MEAN = 9;
40   public final static double HIGH_PROFANITY_MIN = 8;
41   public final static double HIGH_PROFANITY_MAX = 10.9;
42   //probability of rating a contribution
43   public final static int NO_PROFANITY_RATING_PROBABILITY = 20;
44   public final static int AVERAGE_PROFANITY_RATING_PROBABILITY = 30;
45   public final static int HIGH_PROFANITY_RATING_PROBABILITY = 20;
46   //rating score distribution for randomization
47   public final static int RATING_STANDARD_DEVIATION = 2;
48   public final static int RATING_MEAN = 2;
49   public final static double RATING_MIN = 1;
50   public final static double RATING_MAX = 6;
51   //profanity weightings by (m*a+c)
52   public final static double NO_PROFANITY_RATING_WEIGHTING_M = -1;
53   public final static double AVERAGE_PROFANITY_RATING_WEIGHTING_M = -
                   0.5;
54   public final static double HIGH_PROFANITY_RATING_WEIGHTING_M = 1;
55   public final static double NO_PROFANITY_RATING_WEIGHTING_C = 5;
```

```
56   public final static double AVERAGE_PROFANITY_RATING_WEIGHTING_C =
                 2.5;
57   public final static double HIGH_PROFANITY_RATING_WEIGHTING_C = -5;
58   //internal representations
59   public final static int HIGH_PROFANITY = 1;
60   public final static int AVERAGE_PROFANITY = 0;
61   public final static int NO_PROFANITY = -1;
62
63   //variables
64   public static ArrayList<Contribution> contributions;  //Contains all
                 contributions objects in system
65   public static int contributionsLastUpdateStartIndex; //index of beginning of
                 last update
66   public static ArrayList<Rating> ratings;  //Contains all rating objects in
                 system
67   public static int ratingsLastUpdateStartIndex; //index of beginning last
                 update
68   public ArrayList<User> users;  //Contains all user objects in system
69   private ArrayList<Integer> highProfanityUserIndex;  //Contains the index
                 (relative to ArrayList user) of high profanity users
70   private ArrayList<Integer> averageProfanityUserIndex;//Contains the index
                 (relative to ArrayList user) of average profanity users
71   private ArrayList<Integer> noProfanityUserIndex;  //Contains the index
                 (relative to ArrayList user) of low profanity users
72   public double beta; //community socio-technical indicator
73   public double averageA; //community average number of occurrences
74   private static String current_token = null; //data input holder
75   private static StringTokenizer reader;  //data input holder
76
77   public Main() {
78      users = new ArrayList<User>();  //Contains all user objects
79      contributions = new ArrayList<Contribution>(); //Contains all
                 contributions
80      ratings = new ArrayList<Rating>();  //Contains all ratings
81      highProfanityUserIndex = new ArrayList<Integer>(); //Contains the
                 index (relative to ArrayList user) of high profanity users
```

```
82      averageProfanityUserIndex = new ArrayList<Integer>();//Contains the
                        index (relative to ArrayList user) of average profanity
                        users
83      noProfanityUserIndex = new ArrayList<Integer>();//Contains the index
                        (relative to ArrayList user) of low profanity users
84      beta = 1.0;
85      averageA = 1.0;
86    }
87
88    public static void main(String[] args) {
89      int amountHighProfanityUsers, amountNoProfanityUsers,
                        amountAverageProfanityUsers, option;
90      Main simulation = new Main();
91      //users
92      //user calculations and type generation
93      amountHighProfanityUsers = USER_TOTAL * USER_HIGH_PROFANITY /
                        100;
94      amountNoProfanityUsers = USER_TOTAL * USER_NO_PROFANITY /
                        100;
95      amountAverageProfanityUsers = USER_TOTAL -
                        amountHighProfanityUsers -amountNoProfanityUsers;
96      //generate users
97      System.out.println("Generating "+USER_TOTAL+" users:");
98      System.out.println("_"+amountNoProfanityUsers+" no profanity
                        ("+USER_NO_PROFANITY+"%)");
99      System.out.println("_"+amountAverageProfanityUsers+" average
                        profanity ("+(100 - USER_NO_PROFANITY -
                        USER_HIGH_PROFANITY)+"%)");
100     System.out.println("_"+amountHighProfanityUsers+" high profanity
                        ("+USER_HIGH_PROFANITY+"%)\n");
101
                        simulation.generateUsers(amountHighProfanityUsers,HIGH_PROFANITY);
102     simulation.generateUsers(amountAverageProfanityUsers,
                        AVERAGE_PROFANITY);
103     simulation.generateUsers(amountNoProfanityUsers, NO_PROFANITY);
104     for(int i=0;i<USER_TOTAL;i++){
105       simulation.potentiallyContribute(i);
106     }
```

```
107     System.out.flush();
108
109     //simulation loop
110     while(true){
111
                        System.out.println("                                              ")
112     System.out.println("(1) Simulate more contributions + ratings  (2)
                        view contribution data  (3) Exit");
113         int value=0;
114         boolean getInput =true;
115         while(getInput) {
116            System.out.println("option (1-3): ");
117            String token = getNextToken();
118            try{ value = Integer.parseInt (token);
119                getInput =false;
120            }catch (Exception exception){
121                System.out.print("Please enter a valid value, ");
122                value = Integer.MIN_VALUE;
123                getInput =true;
124            }
125         }
126         clearscr();
127         if(value==3){//exit
128            System.exit(1);
129         }
130         if(value==2){ //contribution data
131            //create profanity distribution in contributions
132            System.out.println("Distribution of profanity within
                        contributions:\n");
133            System.out.flush();
134            ArrayList<Integer> profanityList = new
                        ArrayList<Integer>(simulation.getContributions().size());
135            for(int i=0; i<simulation.getContributions().size(); i++)
136                profanityList.add(simulation.getContribution(i).profanity);
137            simulation.listDistribution(profanityList, 0, 10);
138         }
139         else if(value==1){ //continue simulation
```

```
140        for(int j=0; j<20; j++) {
141            simulation.contributionsLastUpdateStartIndex =
                       (simulation.contributions.size()-1);
142            simulation.contributionsLastUpdateStartIndex = (ratings.size()-1);
143            //add ratings
144            System.out.flush();
145            for(int i=0;i<USER_TOTAL;i++){
146                for(int
                         contributionNumber=0;contributionNumber<simulation.getContributionsSize();contributionNumber++)
147                simulation.potentiallyRate(i, contributionNumber); //user i
                       might contributes
148            }
149            simulation.recalculateBeta();
150            System.out.print("\n"+j+" beta:
                       "+(float)((int)(simulation.getBeta()*100))/100);
151            System.out.print("\tavrg. a:
                       "+((float)(int)(simulation.getAverageA()*100))/100);
152            double value1 = simulation.getAverageAlpha(HIGH_PROFANITY);
153            double value2 =
                       simulation.getAverageAlpha(AVERAGE_PROFANITY);
154            double value3 = simulation.getAverageAlpha(NO_PROFANITY);
155            double total = value1+value2+value3;
156            if(total<0){
157                total = total* (-1);
158            }
159            double check = (value1/total) + (value2/total) + (value3/total);
160            System.out.print("\tavrg alpha high: "+((float)(int)((value1/
                       total)*10000))/100);
161            System.out.print("\tavrg alpha average: "+((float)(int)((value2/
                       total)*10000)/100));
162            System.out.print("\tavrg alpha no: "+((float)(int)((value3/
                       total)*10000)/100));
163            System.out.print("\tcheck: "+check);
164            System.out.flush();
165        }
166    }
167 }//execution loop end
```

```
168   }
169
170   //simple clear screen function
171   public static void clearscr(){
172     //clear screen
173     for(int i=0; i<100; i++)
174         System.out.println("\n");
175   }
176
177   //data input function
178   private static BufferedReader in = new BufferedReader
179     (new InputStreamReader(System.in));
180
181   //data input function
182   private static String getNextToken()
183   { return getNextToken (true);
184   }
185
186   //data input function
187   private static String getNextToken (boolean skip)
188   {  String token;
189     if (current_token == null)
190         token = getNextInputToken (skip);
191     else{
192         token = current_token;
193         current_token = null;
194     }
195     return token;
196   }
197
198   //data input function
199   private static String getNextInputToken (boolean skip)
200   {  final String delimiters = " \t\n\r\f";
201     String token = null;
202     try{
203         if (reader == null)
204             reader = new StringTokenizer
```

```
205          (in.readLine(), delimiters, true);
206       while (token == null ||
207            ((delimiters.indexOf (token) >= 0) && skip)){
208          while (!reader.hasMoreTokens())
209             reader = new StringTokenizer
210                (in.readLine(), delimiters,true);
211           token = reader.nextToken(); }}
212       catch (Exception exception)
213       { token = null; }
214       return token;
215    }
216
217    //data input function
218    public static boolean endOfLine()
219    {    return !reader.hasMoreTokens();
220    }
221
222    public ArrayList<Contribution> getContributions(){
223          return contributions;
224    }
225
226    public ArrayList<Rating> getRatings(){
227          return ratings;
228    }
229    //return a user from a user id
230    public User getUser(int id){
231          return users.get(id);
232    }
233
234    //return a contribution from a contribution id
235    public Contribution getContribution(int id){
236       return contributions.get(id);
237
238    }
239    //return a rating from a rating id
240    public Rating getRating(int id){
```

```
241        return ratings.get(id);
242    }
243
244    //add specified number of a specific type of users
245    public void generateUsers(int number, int type){
246       for(int i = 1; i <= number; i++){
247          users.add(new User(type)); //add user
248          users.get(users.size()-1).setId(users.size()-1); //set user id
249          if(type==HIGH_PROFANITY){
250             highProfanityUserIndex.add(users.size()-1);
251          }else if(type==AVERAGE_PROFANITY){
252             averageProfanityUserIndex.add(users.size()-1);
253          }else if(type==NO_PROFANITY){
254             noProfanityUserIndex.add(users.size()-1);
255          }
256       }
257    }
258
259    //lists all users
260    public void listUsers(){
261       if(users.size() == 0)
262          System.out.println("listUsers() says: No Users in System!");
263       else{
264          for(int count =0; count < users.size(); count++)
265             System.out.println("id: " +count+ "\tprofanity type:
                      "+users.get(count).type+"\tprofanity alpha: "
266                +users.get(count).getAlpha());
267       }
268    }
269
270    //lists all users of a specific type
271    public void listUsers(int type){
272       int id =0;
273       if(users.size() == 0)
274          System.out.println("listUsers(int type) says: No Users in System!");
275       else{
276          if(type == HIGH_PROFANITY){
```

```
277        for(int count =0; count < highProfanityUserIndex.size();
                   count++){
278          id = highProfanityUserIndex.get(count);
279          System.out.println("id: " +id+ "\tprofanity type:
                   "+users.get(id).type+"\tprofanity alpha: "
280          +users.get(id).getAlpha());}
281        }else if(type == AVERAGE_PROFANITY){
282          for(int count =0; count < averageProfanityUserIndex.size();
                   count++){
283          id = averageProfanityUserIndex.get(count);
284          System.out.println("id: " +id+ "\tprofanity type:
                   "+users.get(id).type+"\tprofanity alpha: "
285          +users.get(id).getAlpha());}
286        }else if(type == NO_PROFANITY){
287          for(int count =0; count < noProfanityUserIndex.size(); count++){
288          id = noProfanityUserIndex.get(count);
289          System.out.println("id: " +id+ "\tprofanity type:
                   "+users.get(id).type+"\tprofanity alpha: "
290          +users.get(id).getAlpha());}
291        }
292      }
293    }
294
295    //lists all ratings
296    public void listRatings(){
297      if(ratings.size() == 0)
298        System.out.println("listRatings() says: No Ratings in System!");
299      else{
300        for(int contribution =0; contribution < contributions.size();
                   contribution++){
301          System.out.println("id: " +contribution+ "\tprofanity:
                   "+contributions.get(contribution).getProfanity()+"\tNumber
                   of Ratings: "
302          +
                   contributions.get(contribution).getRatingIndex().size()+"\tAverage
                   Rating:
                   "+contributions.get(contribution).getAverageRating()+"\n\trated:");
```

```
303        for(int index=0;
                        index<getContribution(contribution).ratingIndex.size();
                        index++){
304            System.out.println("\tscore:
                        "+getRating(getContribution(contribution).ratingIndex.get(index)).getScore()+"\tby
                        user:
                        "+getRating(getContribution(contribution).ratingIndex.get(index)).getFromUserID());
305            }
306
307        }
308      }
309    }
310
311  /*randomly generates uniformly distributed integers from 0-99 (100%-1) to
                        decide
312   *whether a user rates a post or not.*/
313  public void potentiallyRate(int fromUserID, int contributionID){
314    Random generator = new Random();
315    if(getUser(fromUserID).getType() == HIGH_PROFANITY){
316      if(generator.nextInt(100) <
                        HIGH_PROFANITY_RATING_PROBABILITY)
317        getUser(fromUserID).rate(contributionID);
318      }else if(getUser(fromUserID).getType() == AVERAGE_PROFANITY){
319      if(generator.nextInt(100) <
                        AVERAGE_PROFANITY_RATING_PROBABILITY)
320        getUser(fromUserID).rate(contributionID);
321      }else if(getUser(fromUserID).getType() == NO_PROFANITY){
322      if(generator.nextInt(100) < NO_PROFANITY_RATING_PROBABILITY)
323        getUser(fromUserID).rate(contributionID);
324    }
325    }
326
327
328  /*randomly generates uniformly distributed integers from 0-99 (100%-1) to
                        decide
329   *whether a user posts or not.*/
330  public void potentiallyContribute(int userID){
```

```
331    Random generator = new Random();
332    if(getUser(userID).getType() == HIGH_PROFANITY){
333        if(generator.nextInt(100) <
                        CONTRIBUTION_PROB_HIGH_PROFANITY)
334            getUser(userID).contribute();
335    }else if(getUser(userID).getType() == AVERAGE_PROFANITY){
336        if(generator.nextInt(100) <
                        CONTRIBUTION_PROB_AVERAGE_PROFANITY)
337            getUser(userID).contribute();
338    }else if(getUser(userID).getType() == NO_PROFANITY){
339        if(generator.nextInt(100) < CONTRIBUTION_PROB_NO_PROFANITY)
340            getUser(userID).contribute();
341    }
342    }
343
344    //returns the average number of occurrences in system
345    public double getAverageA(){
346        double average = 0;
347        for(int count =0; count < contributions.size(); count++)
348            average = average + getContribution(count).getProfanity();
349        average /= contributions.size();
350        averageA = average;
351        return average;
352    }
353
354    //print contributions to screen
355    public void listContributions(){
356        if(contributions.size() == 0)
357            System.out.println("listContributions() says: No Contributions in
                        System!");
358        else{
359            for(int count =0; count < contributions.size(); count++)
360                System.out.println("id: " +count+ "\tuser:
                        "+contributions.get(count).getUserID()+" \tprofanity: "
361                    +contributions.get(count).getProfanity());
362        }
363    }
```

```
364
365   //displays an ASCII line graph of a distribution
366   public void listDistribution(ArrayList<Integer> list, int minValue, int
                      maxValue){
367      minValue = maxValue =0;
368      for(int i=0; i<list.size(); i++){
369         if(list.get(i)>maxValue)
370            maxValue = list.get(i);
371         if(list.get(i)<minValue)
372            minValue = list.get(i);
373      }
374      int[] count = new int[maxValue-minValue+1];
375      float[] percentage = new float[maxValue-minValue+1];
376      for(int i=0; i<count.length;i++)   //initialise
377         count[i]=0;
378      for(int i=0; i<list.size(); i++)   //increment
379         count[list.get(i)-minValue]++;
380      for(int i=0; i<count.length;i++)   //convert to percentages
381         percentage[i] = ((count[i]/(float)list.size())*100);
382      for(int i=maxValue; i>=minValue; i—){ //display
383         System.out.print(((int)(percentage[i]*100))/
                      (float)100+"%\t"+i+"\t|");
384         for(int j=0; j<percentage[i]; j++)
385            System.out.print("x");
386         System.out.print("\n");
387      }
388      System.out.println("total: "+list.size());
389   }
390
391   //calculate alpha for all users
392   public void calculateAlpha(){
393      for(int i=0; i<users.size();i++)
394         getUser(i).calculateAlpha();
395   }
396
397   //returns average alpha value for a user group
398   public double getAverageAlpha(int userType){
```

```
399    double average = 0.0;
400    if(userType == HIGH_PROFANITY){
401       for(int index = 0; index < highProfanityUserIndex.size(); index++){
402          average += getUser(index).calculateAlpha();
403       }
404       average /= highProfanityUserIndex.size();
405    }else if(userType == AVERAGE_PROFANITY){
406       for(int index = 0; index < averageProfanityUserIndex.size();
                     index++){
407          average += getUser(index).calculateAlpha();
408       }
409       average /= averageProfanityUserIndex.size();
410
411    }else if(userType == NO_PROFANITY){
412       for(int index = 0; index < noProfanityUserIndex.size(); index++){
413          average += getUser(index).calculateAlpha();
414       }
415       average /= noProfanityUserIndex.size();
416    }
417    return average;
418  }
419
420
421
422  //calculates average m of all contributions, or beta, the community STI
423  public double recalculateBeta(){
424    double average=0.0;
425    double minRating = 1.0;
426    for(int i=0; i<contributions.size();i++){
427       if(getContribution(i).getRatingPerAttributeUnit()< minRating){
428          minRating = getContribution(i).getRatingPerAttributeUnit();
429       }
430    }
431    minRating—;
432    for(int i=0; i<contributions.size();i++){
433       if(!getContribution(i).getRatingIndex().isEmpty()){
```

```
434            average = (average + (1.0 /
                         (getContribution(i).getRatingPerAttributeUnit()-
                         minRating)));
435        }
436      }
437      average = contributions.size() / average;
438      average += minRating;   //shift ratings
439      if(average == 0){
440          return 1;
441      }else{
442          beta = average;
443          return beta;
444      }
445   }
446
447   public double getBeta(){
448      return beta;
449   }
450
451
452
453 /*
454  *_____
455  * USER OBJECT
456  *_____
457  */
458
459   public class User {
460      private int id; //user id, assigned only when added to "users" as id is an
                         index to that object
461      private ArrayList<Integer> contributionIDs;   ///ID of contributions
462      private ArrayList<Integer> ratingsGivenIDs;   ///ID of ratings given
                         contributions
463      private double alpha;//user status
464      private int type;   //type of user
465
466      //create average user
```

```
467     public User() {
468         setContributionIDs(new ArrayList<Integer>());
469         setRatingsGivenIDs(new ArrayList<Integer>());
470         alpha = 1;
471         type = 0;
472     }
473
474     //create user of input type
475     public User(int type) {
476         setContributionIDs(new ArrayList<Integer>());
477         setRatingsGivenIDs(new ArrayList<Integer>());
478         alpha= 1;
479         this.type = type;
480     }
481
482     //returns the average amount of profanity in user's posts
483     public double getAverageProfanity(){
484         double average = 0.0;
485         for(int contribution=0; contribution<contributionIDs.size();
                        contribution++){
486             average +=
                        contributions.get(contributionIDs.get(contribution)).getProfanity();
487         }
488         return (average / contributionIDs.size());
489     }
490
491     //calculates new alpha from all posts and ratings of those posts
492     public double calculateAlpha(){
493         double mb;
494         double aa;
495         int signBit;
496         double f; //change in alpha
497         /*calculate sign bit*/
498         if(beta >= 0)
499             signBit = 1;
500         else{
```

```
501          signBit = -1;
502        }
503      for(int contribution=0; contribution<contributionIDs.size();
                    contribution++){
504        mb =
                    getContribution(contributionIDs.get(contribution)).getAverageRating()
                    / recalculateBeta(); // m/b
505        aa = getAverageProfanity() / getAverageA(); //a/a-bar
506        f = mb * aa * signBit;
507        alpha = alpha + f;
508      }
509      return alpha;
510    }
511
512    //user rates the input contribution
513    public void rate(int contributionID){
514      float randomisation = 0;
515      double weighting = 0.0;
516      int score;
517      Random generator = new Random();
518      //CALCULATE WEIGHTINGS MA+C
519      if(type==NO_PROFANITY){
520        weighting = NO_PROFANITY_RATING_WEIGHTING_M *
                    getContribution(contributionID).getProfanity() +
                    NO_PROFANITY_RATING_WEIGHTING_C;
521      }else if(type==AVERAGE_PROFANITY){
522        weighting = AVERAGE_PROFANITY_RATING_WEIGHTING_M *
                    getContribution(contributionID).getProfanity() +
                    AVERAGE_PROFANITY_RATING_WEIGHTING_C;
523      }else if(type==HIGH_PROFANITY){
524        weighting = HIGH_PROFANITY_RATING_WEIGHTING_M *
                    getContribution(contributionID).getProfanity() +
                    HIGH_PROFANITY_RATING_WEIGHTING_C;
525      }
526      //WEIGHT BY USER ALPHA
527      if(alpha < 0){
528        alpha=alpha*2-alpha;
```

```
529          }
530          score = (int)(weighting * alpha);
531          int index = getContribution(contributionID).rate(score, id);
532          ratingsGivenIDs.add(index); //add rating and index
533      }
534
535      //create a user contribution
536      public void contribute(){
537       Contribution contribution = new Contribution();//create contribution
538       float profanityTemp, lengthOfPostTemp;
539       int profanity=0, lengthOfPost=0;
540       Random generator = new Random();
541       if(type==NO_PROFANITY){
542            profanity = NO_PROFANITY_OCCURENCE;
543          }else if(type==AVERAGE_PROFANITY){
544          //generate contribution attributes
545          while((profanityTemp = (float) generator.nextGaussian()*
                        AVERAGE_PROFANITY_STANDARD_DEVIATION +
                        AVERAGE_PROFANITY_MEAN) >
                        AVERAGE_PROFANITY_MAX || profanityTemp <
                        AVERAGE_PROFANITY_MIN);
546          profanity = (int)(profanityTemp); //scale + translate
547          }
548          else{
549          //generate contribution attributes
550          while((profanityTemp = (float) generator.nextGaussian()*
                        HIGH_PROFANITY_STANDARD_DEVIATION +
                        HIGH_PROFANITY_MEAN) > HIGH_PROFANITY_MAX
                        || profanityTemp < HIGH_PROFANITY_MIN);
551          profanity = (int)(profanityTemp); //scale + translate
552          }
553          /*add contribution*/
554          contribution.setProfanity(profanity);   //profanity
555          contribution.setId(contributions.size()+1); //id
556          contribution.setUserID(id);
557          contributions.add(contribution); //add contribution
```

```
558            getContributionIDs().add(contributions.size()); //index contribution
                        with user
559      }
560
561      public int getId() {
562          return id;
563      }
564
565      public void setId(int id) {
566          this.id = id;
567      }
568
569      public ArrayList<Integer> getContributionIDs() {
570          return contributionIDs;
571      }
572
573      public void setContributionIDs(ArrayList<Integer> contributionIDs) {
574          this.contributionIDs = contributionIDs;
575      }
576
577      public double getAlpha() {
578          return alpha;
579      }
580
581      public void setAlpha(double alpha) {
582          this.alpha = alpha;
583      }
584
585      public int getType() {
586          return type;
587      }
588
589      public void setType(int type) {
590          this.type = type;
591      }
592
593      public ArrayList<Integer> getRatingsGivenIDs() {
```

```
594        return ratingsGivenIDs;
595    }
596
597    public void setRatingsGivenIDs(ArrayList<Integer> ratingsGivenIDs) {
598        this.ratingsGivenIDs = ratingsGivenIDs;
599    }
600
601
602 }//end of User class
603
604
605
606
607 /*
608  *_____
609  * CONTRIBUTION OBJECT
610  *_____
611  */
612    public class Contribution {
613        private int id;        //id of contribution
614        private int userID;     //id of user who posted contribution
615        private int profanity;  //amount of profanity (a) within contribution
616        private ArrayList<Integer> ratingIndex;
617
618        public Contribution() {
619            ratingIndex = new ArrayList<Integer>();
620        }
621
622        //returns id of the rating
623        private int addRating(int score, int fromUserID){
624            ratings.add(new Rating(score, id, fromUserID));
625            int ratingid = ratings.size()-1;
626            ratingIndex.add(ratingid); //keep track locally
627            return ratingid;
628        }
629
630        //returns id of the rating
```

```
631        public int rate(int score, int fromUserID){
632            return addRating(score, fromUserID);
633        }
634
635        public double getAverageRating(){
636            double average=0.0;
637            for(int i=0; i<ratingIndex.size(); i++){
638                average = average + ratings.get(ratingIndex.get(i)).getScore();
639            }
640            return (average / ratingIndex.size());
641        }
642
643        //returns m = r-bar/ai,j
644        public double getRatingPerAttributeUnit(){
645            return (getAverageRating()/(profanity)); //BUG FIX: profanity now never
                            0

646
647        }
648
649        public int getId() {
650            return id;
651        }
652
653        public void setId(int id) {
654            this.id = id;
655        }
656
657        public int getProfanity() {
658            return profanity;
659        }
660
661        public void setProfanity(int profanity) {
662            this.profanity = profanity;
663        }
664
665        public int getUserID() {
```

```
666          return userID;
667      }
668
669      public void setUserID(int userID) {
670          this.userID = userID;
671      }
672
673      public ArrayList<Integer> getRatingIndex() {
674          return ratingIndex;
675      }
676
677      public void setRatingIndex(ArrayList<Integer> ratingIndex) {
678          this.ratingIndex = ratingIndex;
679      }
680
681  }//end Contribution class
682
683
684
685 /*
686  *————————————————————————————
687  * RATING OBJECT
688  *————————————————————————————
689  */
690
691  public class Rating{
692      private int fromUserID;
693      private int contributionID;
694      private int score;
695
696      public Rating(int score, int contribution, int fromUserID){
697          this.fromUserID = fromUserID;
698          this.score = score;
699      }
700
701      public int getFromUserID() {
702          return fromUserID;
```

```
703     }
704
705     public void setFromUserID(int fromUserID) {
706         this.fromUserID = fromUserID;
707     }
708
709     public int getScore() {
710         return score;
711     }
712
713     public void setScore(int score) {
714         this.score = score;
715     }
716
717     public int getContributionID() {
718         return contributionID;
719     }
720
721     public void setContributionID(int contributionID) {
722         this.contributionID = contributionID;
723     }
724 }
725
726   public ArrayList<Integer> getHighProfanityUserIndex() {
727       return highProfanityUserIndex;
728   }
729
730   public void setHighProfanityUserIndex(ArrayList<Integer>
                        highProfanityUserIndex) {
731     this.highProfanityUserIndex = highProfanityUserIndex;
732   }
733
734   public ArrayList<Integer> getAverageProfanityUserIndex() {
735       return averageProfanityUserIndex;
736   }
737
```

```
738    public void setAverageProfanityUserIndex(ArrayList<Integer>
                       averageProfanityUserIndex) {
739       this.averageProfanityUserIndex = averageProfanityUserIndex;
740    }
741
742    public ArrayList<Integer> getNoProfanityUserIndex() {
743       return noProfanityUserIndex;
744    }
745
746    public void setNoProfanityUserIndex(ArrayList<Integer>
                       noProfanityUserIndex) {
747       this.noProfanityUserIndex = noProfanityUserIndex;
748    }
749 }
```

APPENDIX 2
Simulation Output

Simulation info:
Size: 744 lines
Time taken to run through first 20 iterations of simulation:
approximately 4 minutes on a Pentium 4, 2.8 GHz, with 512mb
RAM

Minus means low status
Positive alpha means positive status

_____

DATA USED:
_____

```
//user data
  public final static int USER_TOTAL = 300;        //number of
users to generate
  public final static int USER_HIGH_PROFANITY = 20;   //
percentage of high profanity users
  public final static int USER_NO_PROFANITY = 20;     //
percentage of no profanity users
  //profanity definitions
```

note: the above data are changed in each of the three simulations
(A, B, C)

```
//interaction data
  public final static int
CONTRIBUTION_PROB_HIGH_PROFANITY = 20;   // %
```

probability of a high profanity user posting
    public final static int
CONTRIBUTION_PROB_AVERAGE_PROFANITY = 60; // %
probability of a avrg profanity user posting
    public final static int CONTRIBUTION_PROB_NO_PROFANITY
= 20;   // % probability of a no profanity user posting
    //profanity actual occurrence probability distribution
    public final static int NO_PROFANITY_OCCURENCE = 1; //
lowest profanity occurrences value
    public final static float
AVERAGE_PROFANITY_STANDARD_DEVIATION = (float)2.5;
    public final static float AVERAGE_PROFANITY_MEAN = 4;
    public final static double AVERAGE_PROFANITY_MIN = 1;
    public final static double AVERAGE_PROFANITY_MAX = 7.9;
    public final static float
HIGH_PROFANITY_STANDARD_DEVIATION = (float)1.0;
    public final static float HIGH_PROFANITY_MEAN = 9;
    public final static double HIGH_PROFANITY_MIN = 8;
    public final static double HIGH_PROFANITY_MAX = 10.9;
    //probability of rating a contribution
    public final static int NO_PROFANITY_RATING_PROBABILITY
= 20; // percentage chance of a user rating a post
    public final static int
AVERAGE_PROFANITY_RATING_PROBABILITY = 30; //
percentage chance of a user rating a post
    public final static int
HIGH_PROFANITY_RATING_PROBABILITY = 20; // percentage
chance of a user rating a post
    //rating score distribution for randomization
    public final static int RATING_STANDARD_DEVIATION = 2;
    public final static int RATING_MEAN = 2;
    public final static double RATING_MIN = 1;
    public final static double RATING_MAX = 6;
    //profanity weightings by (m*a+c)
    public final static double
NO_PROFANITY_RATING_WEIGHTING_M = -1;
    public final static double
AVERAGE_PROFANITY_RATING_WEIGHTING_M = -0.5;

```
    public final static double
HIGH_PROFANITY_RATING_WEIGHTING_M = 1;
    public final static double
NO_PROFANITY_RATING_WEIGHTING_C = 5;
    public final static double
AVERAGE_PROFANITY_RATING_WEIGHTING_C = 2.5;
    public final static double
HIGH_PROFANITY_RATING_WEIGHTING_C = -5;
```

A TRIAL 1

```
beta  (community STI) : 0.17     avrg. a: 4.16
beta  (community STI) : 0.26     avrg. a: 4.16
beta  (community STI) : 0.37     avrg. a: 4.16
beta  (community STI) : 0.48     avrg. a: 4.16
beta  (community STI) : 0.5      avrg. a: 4.16
beta  (community STI) : 0.47     avrg. a: 4.16
beta  (community STI) : 0.55     avrg. a: 4.16
beta  (community STI) : 0.54     avrg. a: 4.16
beta  (community STI) : 0.67     avrg. a: 4.16
beta  (community STI) : 0.6      avrg. a: 4.16
beta  (community STI) : 0.56     avrg. a: 4.16
beta  (community STI) : -0.88    avrg. a: 4.16
beta  (community STI) : -0.49    avrg. a: 4.16
beta  (community STI) : -1.35    avrg. a: 4.16
beta  (community STI) : -2.75    avrg. a: 4.16
beta  (community STI) : -1.66    avrg. a: 4.16
beta  (community STI) : -3.08    avrg. a: 4.16
beta  (community STI) : -6.29    avrg. a: 4.16
beta  (community STI) : -6.29    avrg. a: 4.16
beta  (community STI) : -6.81    avrg. a: 4.16
```

avrg alpha high: -14.63   avrg alpha average: 0.25
avrg alpha high: -30.95   avrg alpha average: -10.78
avrg alpha high: -36.0   avrg alpha average: -12.27
avrg alpha high: -37.31   avrg alpha average: -12.93
avrg alpha high: -37.99   avrg alpha average: -13.28
avrg alpha high: -37.98   avrg alpha average: -13.47
avrg alpha high: -38.84   avrg alpha average: -13.65
avrg alpha high: -38.62   avrg alpha average: -13.73
avrg alpha high: -39.53   avrg alpha average: -13.75
avrg alpha high: -39.66   avrg alpha average: -13.69
avrg alpha high: -39.39   avrg alpha average: -13.68
avrg alpha high: -40.75   avrg alpha average: -13.72
avrg alpha high: -39.21   avrg alpha average: -13.68
avrg alpha high: -41.59   avrg alpha average: -13.7
avrg alpha high: -42.35   avrg alpha average: -13.7
avrg alpha high: -41.83   avrg alpha average: -13.66
avrg alpha high: -42.37   avrg alpha average: -13.64
avrg alpha high: -42.74   avrg alpha average: -13.64
avrg alpha high: -42.71   avrg alpha average: -13.64
avrg alpha high: -42.72   avrg alpha average: -13.63

avrg alpha no: -85.61   check: -1.0
avrg alpha no: -58.25   check: -1.0
avrg alpha no: -51.71   check: -1.0
avrg alpha no: -49.75   check: -1.0
avrg alpha no: -48.72   check: -1.0
avrg alpha no: -48.54   check: -1.0
avrg alpha no: -47.5   check: -0.9999999999999998
avrg alpha no: -47.63   check: -1.0
avrg alpha no: -46.7   check: -1.0
avrg alpha no: -46.64   check: -1.0
avrg alpha no: -46.91   check: -1.0

avrg alpha no: -45.51   check: -1.0
avrg alpha no: -47.1   check: -1.0000000000000002
avrg alpha no: -44.69   check: -1.0
avrg alpha no: -43.93   check: -1.0
avrg alpha no: -44.49   check: -1.0
avrg alpha no: -43.97   check: -0.9999999999999999
avrg alpha no: -43.61   check: -1.0
avrg alpha no: -43.64   check: -1.0
avrg alpha no: -43.63   check: -1.0

---

(1) view system data (2) view contribution data (3) view rating data
(4) Simulate more contributions + ratings (9) Exit
option (1-3):

A TRIAL 2

---

0 beta: 0.16   avrg. a: 4.03
1 beta: 0.4   avrg. a: 4.03
2 beta: 0.56   avrg. a: 4.03
3 beta: 0.55   avrg. a: 4.03
4 beta: 0.81   avrg. a: 4.03
5 beta: 0.74   avrg. a: 4.03
6 beta: 0.44   avrg. a: 4.03
7 beta: 1.17   avrg. a: 4.03
8 beta: 0.38   avrg. a: 4.03
9 beta: -0.09   avrg. a: 4.03
10 beta: -2.93   avrg. a: 4.03
11 beta: -9.63   avrg. a: 4.03
12 beta: -12.04   avrg. a: 4.03
13 beta: -16.7   avrg. a: 4.03
14 beta: -21.14   avrg. a: 4.03
15 beta: -28.3   avrg. a: 4.03

16 beta: -32.89   avrg. a: 4.03
17 beta: -36.25   avrg. a: 4.03
18 beta: -38.88   avrg. a: 4.03
19 beta: -44.9   avrg. a: 4.03

avrg alpha high: -18.11   avrg alpha average: -7.08
avrg alpha high: -32.95   avrg alpha average: -11.35
avrg alpha high: -35.38   avrg alpha average: -12.29
avrg alpha high: -36.28   avrg alpha average: -12.74
avrg alpha high: -38.74   avrg alpha average: -12.86
avrg alpha high: -38.32   avrg alpha average: -12.95
avrg alpha high: -36.39   avrg alpha average: -12.94
avrg alpha high: -40.46   avrg alpha average: -13.07
avrg alpha high: -35.96   avrg alpha average: -13.0
avrg alpha high: -30.0   avrg alpha average: -12.86
avrg alpha high: -42.74   avrg alpha average: -13.18
avrg alpha high: -43.12   avrg alpha average: -13.18
avrg alpha high: -43.13   avrg alpha average: -13.18
avrg alpha high: -43.18   avrg alpha average: -13.18
avrg alpha high: -43.2   avrg alpha average: -13.18
avrg alpha high: -43.23   avrg alpha average: -13.18
avrg alpha high: -43.24   avrg alpha average: -13.18
avrg alpha high: -43.25   avrg alpha average: -13.18
avrg alpha high: -43.25   avrg alpha average: -13.18
avrg alpha high: -43.26   avrg alpha average: -13.18

avrg alpha no: -74.8   check: -1.0
avrg alpha no: -55.68   check: -1.0
avrg alpha no: -52.31   check: -1.0000000000000002
avrg alpha no: -50.97   check: -1.0
avrg alpha no: -48.39   check: -1.0
avrg alpha no: -48.72   check: -1.0
avrg alpha no: -50.66   check: -0.9999999999999999

avrg alpha no: -46.46   check: -1.0
avrg alpha no: -51.03   check: -1.0
avrg alpha no: -57.12   check: -1.0
avrg alpha no: -44.07   check: -1.0
avrg alpha no: -43.68   check: -1.0
avrg alpha no: -43.67   check: -1.0
avrg alpha no: -43.63   check: -1.0
avrg alpha no: -43.6   check: -1.0
avrg alpha no: -43.57   check: -1.0
avrg alpha no: -43.56   check: -1.0
avrg alpha no: -43.56   check: -0.9999999999999999
avrg alpha no: -43.55   check: -1.0
avrg alpha no: -43.54   check: -1.0

---

(1) view system data (2) view contribution data (3) view rating data
(4) Simulate more contributions + ratings (9) Exit
option (1-3):

A TRIAL 3

---

0 beta: 0.18   avrg. a: 3.85
1 beta: 0.32   avrg. a: 3.85
2 beta: 0.44   avrg. a: 3.85
3 beta: 0.53   avrg. a: 3.85
4 beta: 0.64   avrg. a: 3.85
5 beta: 0.74   avrg. a: 3.85
6 beta: 0.79   avrg. a: 3.85
7 beta: 1.02   avrg. a: 3.85
8 beta: 0.78   avrg. a: 3.85

9 beta: 1.16   avrg. a: 3.85
10 beta: 0.87   avrg. a: 3.85
11 beta: 1.14   avrg. a: 3.85
12 beta: 0.97   avrg. a: 3.85
13 beta: 0.55   avrg. a: 3.85
14 beta: 0.69   avrg. a: 3.85
15 beta: 1.31   avrg. a: 3.85
16 beta: 1.49   avrg. a: 3.85
17 beta: 2.02   avrg. a: 3.85
18 beta: 1.39   avrg. a: 3.85
19 beta: 0.29   avrg. a: 3.85

avrg alpha high: -14.22   avrg alpha average: -1.55
avrg alpha high: -34.06   avrg alpha average: -10.13
avrg alpha high: -37.01   avrg alpha average: -11.75
avrg alpha high: -37.59   avrg alpha average: -12.31
avrg alpha high: -38.99   avrg alpha average: -12.59
avrg alpha high: -39.8   avrg alpha average: -12.78
avrg alpha high: -40.34   avrg alpha average: -12.84
avrg alpha high: -40.83   avrg alpha average: -12.93
avrg alpha high: -40.11   avrg alpha average: -13.1
avrg alpha high: -41.01   avrg alpha average: -13.2
avrg alpha high: -40.56   avrg alpha average: -13.21
avrg alpha high: -41.34   avrg alpha average: -13.22
avrg alpha high: -41.04   avrg alpha average: -13.19
avrg alpha high: -39.72   avrg alpha average: -13.11
avrg alpha high: -40.54   avrg alpha average: -13.13
avrg alpha high: -41.8   avrg alpha average: -13.17
avrg alpha high: -41.99   avrg alpha average: -13.17
avrg alpha high: -42.33   avrg alpha average: -13.16
avrg alpha high: -41.78   avrg alpha average: -13.13
avrg alpha high: -37.68   avrg alpha average: -13.08

avrg alpha no: -84.22   check: -0.9999999999999999
avrg alpha no: -55.79   check: -1.0
avrg alpha no: -51.22   check: -1.0
avrg alpha no: -50.08   check: -1.0
avrg alpha no: -48.41   check: -0.9999999999999999
avrg alpha no: -47.4   check: -1.0
avrg alpha no: -46.81   check: -1.0
avrg alpha no: -46.23   check: -1.0
avrg alpha no: -46.77   check: -1.0
avrg alpha no: -45.78   check: -1.0
avrg alpha no: -46.22   check: -1.0
avrg alpha no: -45.42   check: -1.0
avrg alpha no: -45.76   check: -1.0
avrg alpha no: -47.15   check: -1.0
avrg alpha no: -46.31   check: -1.0000000000000002
avrg alpha no: -45.01   check: -1.0
avrg alpha no: -44.82   check: -1.0
avrg alpha no: -44.5   check: -1.0
avrg alpha no: -45.07   check: -0.9999999999999999
avrg alpha no: -49.23   check: -1.0

---

(1) view system data (2) view contribution data (3) view rating
data
(4) Simulate more contributions + ratings (9) Exit
option (1-3):

MOVING 10% OUT OF HIGH AND INTO AVERAGE

B TRIAL 1

0 beta: 0.33	avrg. a: 3.43
1 beta: 0.4	avrg. a: 3.43
2 beta: 0.48	avrg. a: 3.43
3 beta: 0.55	avrg. a: 3.43
4 beta: 0.63	avrg. a: 3.43
5 beta: 0.68	avrg. a: 3.43
6 beta: 0.75	avrg. a: 3.43
7 beta: 0.82	avrg. a: 3.43
8 beta: 0.89	avrg. a: 3.43
9 beta: 0.93	avrg. a: 3.43
10 beta: 0.96	avrg. a: 3.43
11 beta: 1.04	avrg. a: 3.43
12 beta: 1.09	avrg. a: 3.43
13 beta: 1.08	avrg. a: 3.43
14 beta: 1.19	avrg. a: 3.43
15 beta: 1.15	avrg. a: 3.43
16 beta: 1.19	avrg. a: 3.43
17 beta: 1.28	avrg. a: 3.43
18 beta: 1.32	avrg. a: 3.43
19 beta: 1.29	avrg. a: 3.43

avrg alpha high: 7.59	avrg alpha average: 140.61
avrg alpha high: -75.18	avrg alpha average: 29.41
avrg alpha high: -68.97	avrg alpha average: 12.43
avrg alpha high: -66.09	avrg alpha average: 6.88
avrg alpha high: -65.45	avrg alpha average: 4.55
avrg alpha high: -65.12	avrg alpha average: 3.38

avrg alpha high: -64.72   avrg alpha average: 2.61
avrg alpha high: -64.69   avrg alpha average: 2.12
avrg alpha high: -64.59   avrg alpha average: 1.74
avrg alpha high: -65.05   avrg alpha average: 1.52
avrg alpha high: -64.89   avrg alpha average: 1.33
avrg alpha high: -64.68   avrg alpha average: 1.02
avrg alpha high: -64.73   avrg alpha average: 0.74
avrg alpha high: -65.04   avrg alpha average: 0.64
avrg alpha high: -65.25   avrg alpha average: 0.54
avrg alpha high: -65.46   avrg alpha average: 0.52
avrg alpha high: -65.48   avrg alpha average: 0.42
avrg alpha high: -65.71   avrg alpha average: 0.35
avrg alpha high: -66.01   avrg alpha average: 0.38
avrg alpha high: -66.18   avrg alpha average: 0.47

avrg alpha no: -48.2   check: 0.9999999999999999
avrg alpha no: -54.22   check: -1.0
avrg alpha no: -43.46   check: -1.0
avrg alpha no: -40.79   check: -1.0
avrg alpha no: -39.1   check: -0.9999999999999998
avrg alpha no: -38.26   check: -1.0
avrg alpha no: -37.89   check: -0.9999999999999999
avrg alpha no: -37.42   check: -0.9999999999999999
avrg alpha no: -37.14   check: -1.0
avrg alpha no: -36.47   check: -0.9999999999999999
avrg alpha no: -36.44   check: -1.0
avrg alpha no: -36.33   check: -1.0
avrg alpha no: -36.0   check: -1.0
avrg alpha no: -35.6   check: -0.9999999999999999
avrg alpha no: -35.29   check: -1.0
avrg alpha no: -35.05   check: -1.0
avrg alpha no: -34.93   check: -1.0

avrg alpha no: -34.64   check: -1.0
avrg alpha no: -34.36   check: -1.0
avrg alpha no: -34.28   check: -1.0

---

(1) view system data (2) view contribution data (3) view rating data
(4) Simulate more contributions + ratings (9) Exit
option (1-3):

B TRIAL 2

---

0 beta: 0.19   avrg. a: 4.0
1 beta: 0.28   avrg. a: 4.0
2 beta: 0.4   avrg. a: 4.0
3 beta: 0.5   avrg. a: 4.0
4 beta: 0.53   avrg. a: 4.0
5 beta: 0.65   avrg. a: 4.0
6 beta: 0.72   avrg. a: 4.0
7 beta: 0.83   avrg. a: 4.0
8 beta: 0.95   avrg. a: 4.0
9 beta: 0.84   avrg. a: 4.0
10 beta: 0.91   avrg. a: 4.0
11 beta: 1.06   avrg. a: 4.0
12 beta: 1.04   avrg. a: 4.0
13 beta: 1.05   avrg. a: 4.0
14 beta: 1.26   avrg. a: 4.0
15 beta: 1.34   avrg. a: 4.0
16 beta: 1.15   avrg. a: 4.0
17 beta: 1.33   avrg. a: 4.0
18 beta: 0.55   avrg. a: 4.0
19 beta: 1.05   avrg. a: 4.0

avrg alpha high: -45.22   avrg alpha average: 14.06
avrg alpha high: -57.4   avrg alpha average: -2.7
avrg alpha high: -61.78   avrg alpha average: -4.16
avrg alpha high: -62.49   avrg alpha average: -4.81
avrg alpha high: -62.11   avrg alpha average: -5.28
avrg alpha high: -62.92   avrg alpha average: -5.51
avrg alpha high: -63.38   avrg alpha average: -5.65
avrg alpha high: -63.59   avrg alpha average: -5.77
avrg alpha high: -64.26   avrg alpha average: -5.8
avrg alpha high: -64.21   avrg alpha average: -5.82
avrg alpha high: -64.42   avrg alpha average: -5.83
avrg alpha high: -64.33   avrg alpha average: -5.88
avrg alpha high: -63.93   avrg alpha average: -5.98
avrg alpha high: -63.88   avrg alpha average: -6.09
avrg alpha high: -64.13   avrg alpha average: -6.17
avrg alpha high: -64.21   avrg alpha average: -6.21
avrg alpha high: -64.08   avrg alpha average: -6.23
avrg alpha high: -64.44   avrg alpha average: -6.21
avrg alpha high: -62.93   avrg alpha average: -6.24
avrg alpha high: -64.3   avrg alpha average: -6.21

avrg alpha no: -68.84   check: -1.0
avrg alpha no: -39.89   check: -1.0000000000000002
avrg alpha no: -34.05   check: -1.0
avrg alpha no: -32.69   check: -1.0
avrg alpha no: -32.59   check: -1.0
avrg alpha no: -31.55   check: -0.9999999999999999
avrg alpha no: -30.96   check: -1.0
avrg alpha no: -30.62   check: -1.0
avrg alpha no: -29.93   check: -1.0
avrg alpha no: -29.95   check: -1.0
avrg alpha no: -29.73   check: -0.9999999999999999

avrg alpha no: -29.77   check: -1.0
avrg alpha no: -30.07   check: -1.0
avrg alpha no: -30.01   check: -1.0
avrg alpha no: -29.69   check: -1.0
avrg alpha no: -29.56   check: -1.0
avrg alpha no: -29.67   check: -1.0
avrg alpha no: -29.34   check: -0.9999999999999998
avrg alpha no: -30.81   check: -1.0
avrg alpha no: -29.48   check: -1.0

(1) view system data (2) view contribution data (3) view rating data
(4) Simulate more contributions + ratings (9) Exit
option (1-3):

B TRIAL 3

---

0 beta: 0.22   avrg. a: 3.85
1 beta: 0.36   avrg. a: 3.85
2 beta: 0.47   avrg. a: 3.85
3 beta: 0.62   avrg. a: 3.85
4 beta: 0.69   avrg. a: 3.85
5 beta: 0.86   avrg. a: 3.85
6 beta: 0.97   avrg. a: 3.85
7 beta: 1.0   avrg. a: 3.85
8 beta: 1.37   avrg. a: 3.85
9 beta: 1.6   avrg. a: 3.85
10 beta: 1.81   avrg. a: 3.85
11 beta: 1.9   avrg. a: 3.85
12 beta: 1.8   avrg. a: 3.85
13 beta: 0.97   avrg. a: 3.85
14 beta: 1.72   avrg. a: 3.85

15 beta: 2.24   avrg. a: 3.85
16 beta: 1.49   avrg. a: 3.85
17 beta: 1.08   avrg. a: 3.85
18 beta: 0.0   avrg. a: 3.85
19 beta: -57.91   avrg. a: 3.85

avrg alpha high: -40.86   avrg alpha average: 3.47
avrg alpha high: -55.49   avrg alpha average: -4.1
avrg alpha high: -57.94   avrg alpha average: -5.45
avrg alpha high: -59.01   avrg alpha average: -5.9
avrg alpha high: -59.14   avrg alpha average: -6.24
avrg alpha high: -60.08   avrg alpha average: -6.44
avrg alpha high: -60.43   avrg alpha average: -6.56
avrg alpha high: -60.8   avrg alpha average: -6.63
avrg alpha high: -61.54   avrg alpha average: -6.65
avrg alpha high: -61.89   avrg alpha average: -6.63
avrg alpha high: -62.07   avrg alpha average: -6.63
avrg alpha high: -62.28   avrg alpha average: -6.6
avrg alpha high: -62.35   avrg alpha average: -6.55
avrg alpha high: -61.39   avrg alpha average: -6.51
avrg alpha high: -62.88   avrg alpha average: -6.43
avrg alpha high: -63.21   avrg alpha average: -6.39
avrg alpha high: -62.61   avrg alpha average: -6.38
avrg alpha high: -62.15   avrg alpha average: -6.36
avrg alpha high: -40.62   avrg alpha average: -6.61
avrg alpha high: -64.39   avrg alpha average: -6.26

avrg alpha no: -62.61   check: -1.0
avrg alpha no: -40.4   check: -1.0
avrg alpha no: -36.59   check: -1.0
avrg alpha no: -35.07   check: -1.0
avrg alpha no: -34.6   check: -1.0

avrg alpha no: -33.47   check: -1.0
avrg alpha no: -33.0   check: -1.0
avrg alpha no: -32.56   check: -1.0
avrg alpha no: -31.8   check: -1.0
avrg alpha no: -31.46   check: -1.0
avrg alpha no: -31.29   check: -1.0
avrg alpha no: -31.11   check: -1.0
avrg alpha no: -31.08   check: -1.0
avrg alpha no: -32.08   check: -1.0
avrg alpha no: -30.67   check: -1.0
avrg alpha no: -30.38   check: -0.9999999999999998
avrg alpha no: -30.99   check: -1.0
avrg alpha no: -31.47   check: -1.0
avrg alpha no: -52.75   check: -1.0
avrg alpha no: -29.33   check: -0.9999999999999999

---

(1) view system data (2) view contribution data
(3) view rating data
(4) Simulate more contributions + ratings (9) Exit

MOVING THE 10% OUT OF AVERAGE AND INTO LOW

C TRIAL 1

0 beta: 0.29   avrg. a: 3.74
1 beta: 0.42   avrg. a: 3.74
2 beta: 0.52   avrg. a: 3.74
3 beta: 0.66   avrg. a: 3.74
4 beta: 0.63   avrg. a: 3.74

5 beta: 0.74   avrg. a: 3.74
6 beta: 0.84   avrg. a: 3.74
7 beta: 0.9   avrg. a: 3.74
8 beta: 0.93   avrg. a: 3.74
9 beta: 0.92   avrg. a: 3.74
10 beta: 1.12   avrg. a: 3.74
11 beta: 1.38   avrg. a: 3.74
12 beta: 0.93   avrg. a: 3.74
13 beta: 1.31   avrg. a: 3.74
14 beta: 1.16   avrg. a: 3.74
15 beta: 1.62   avrg. a: 3.74
16 beta: 0.76   avrg. a: 3.74
17 beta: 1.29   avrg. a: 3.74
18 beta: 1.46   avrg. a: 3.74
19 beta: 2.1   avrg. a: 3.74

avrg alpha high: -58.85   avrg alpha average: 8.12
avrg alpha high: -65.62   avrg alpha average: -5.81
avrg alpha high: -65.89   avrg alpha average: -7.59
avrg alpha high: -67.69   avrg alpha average: -7.85
avrg alpha high: -66.75   avrg alpha average: -8.3
avrg alpha high: -66.53   avrg alpha average: -8.68
avrg alpha high: -66.78   avrg alpha average: -8.87
avrg alpha high: -66.61   avrg alpha average: -9.08
avrg alpha high: -66.95   avrg alpha average: -9.11
avrg alpha high: -66.88   avrg alpha average: -9.12
avrg alpha high: -67.13   avrg alpha average: -9.15
avrg alpha high: -67.58   avrg alpha average: -9.15
avrg alpha high: -66.67   avrg alpha average: -9.33
avrg alpha high: -67.69   avrg alpha average: -9.26
avrg alpha high: -67.52   avrg alpha average: -9.3
avrg alpha high: -68.26   avrg alpha average: -9.23

avrg alpha high: -67.04   avrg alpha average: -9.34
avrg alpha high: -68.14   avrg alpha average: -9.23
avrg alpha high: -68.4   avrg alpha average: -9.17
avrg alpha high: -68.74   avrg alpha average: -9.13

avrg alpha no: -49.27   check: -1.0
avrg alpha no: -28.56   check: -1.0
avrg alpha no: -26.5   check: -1.0
avrg alpha no: -24.45   check: -1.0
avrg alpha no: -24.94   check: -1.0
avrg alpha no: -24.77   check: -1.0
avrg alpha no: -24.33   check: -1.0
avrg alpha no: -24.3   check: -1.0000000000000002
avrg alpha no: -23.93   check: -0.9999999999999999
avrg alpha no: -23.99   check: -1.0
avrg alpha no: -23.7   check: -1.0
avrg alpha no: -23.25   check: -0.9999999999999999
avrg alpha no: -23.98   check: -1.0
avrg alpha no: -23.04   check: -1.0
avrg alpha no: -23.16   check: -1.0
avrg alpha no: -22.5   check: -1.0
avrg alpha no: -23.6   check: -1.0
avrg alpha no: -22.62   check: -0.9999999999999998
avrg alpha no: -22.41   check: -1.0
avrg alpha no: -22.11   check: -0.9999999999999999

C TRIAL 2

---

0 beta: 0.3   avrg. a: 3.63
1 beta: 0.47   avrg. a: 3.63
2 beta: 0.64   avrg. a: 3.63

3 beta: 0.83   avrg. a: 3.63
4 beta: 0.84   avrg. a: 3.63
5 beta: 1.08   avrg. a: 3.63
6 beta: 1.07   avrg. a: 3.63
7 beta: 1.22   avrg. a: 3.63
8 beta: 1.36   avrg. a: 3.63
9 beta: 1.52   avrg. a: 3.63
10 beta: 1.36   avrg. a: 3.63
11 beta: 1.62   avrg. a: 3.63
12 beta: 1.93   avrg. a: 3.63
13 beta: 1.92   avrg. a: 3.63
14 beta: 2.1   avrg. a: 3.63
15 beta: 1.94   avrg. a: 3.63
16 beta: 2.37   avrg. a: 3.63
17 beta: 1.9   avrg. a: 3.63
18 beta: 2.04   avrg. a: 3.63
19 beta: 1.98   avrg. a: 3.63

avrg alpha high: -90.51   avrg alpha average: 37.51
avrg alpha high: -72.44   avrg alpha average: -1.88
avrg alpha high: -76.55   avrg alpha average: -3.29
avrg alpha high: -76.21   avrg alpha average: -3.62
avrg alpha high: -75.23   avrg alpha average: -4.31
avrg alpha high: -75.42   avrg alpha average: -4.66
avrg alpha high: -74.49   avrg alpha average: -5.17
avrg alpha high: -74.42   avrg alpha average: -5.54
avrg alpha high: -74.14   avrg alpha average: -5.82
avrg alpha high: -73.97   avrg alpha average: -6.06
avrg alpha high: -73.77   avrg alpha average: -6.21
avrg alpha high: -74.04   avrg alpha average: -6.25
avrg alpha high: -73.99   avrg alpha average: -6.33
avrg alpha high: -73.95   avrg alpha average: -6.38

avrg alpha high: -73.89   avrg alpha average: -6.44
avrg alpha high: -73.73   avrg alpha average: -6.49
avrg alpha high: -73.87   avrg alpha average: -6.52
avrg alpha high: -73.68   avrg alpha average: -6.55
avrg alpha high: -73.76   avrg alpha average: -6.54
avrg alpha high: -73.56   avrg alpha average: -6.58

avrg alpha no: -46.99   check: -1.0
avrg alpha no: -25.66   check: -1.0
avrg alpha no: -20.14   check: -1.0
avrg alpha no: -20.15   check: -1.0
avrg alpha no: -20.45   check: -1.0
avrg alpha no: -19.9   check: -1.0
avrg alpha no: -20.32   check: -1.0
avrg alpha no: -20.03   check: -0.9999999999999999
avrg alpha no: -20.02   check: -1.0
avrg alpha no: -19.95   check: -1.0
avrg alpha no: -20.0   check: -1.0
avrg alpha no: -19.7   check: -1.0
avrg alpha no: -19.67   check: -1.0
avrg alpha no: -19.65   check: -1.0
avrg alpha no: -19.66   check: -1.0
avrg alpha no: -19.76   check: -0.9999999999999999
avrg alpha no: -19.59   check: -1.0
avrg alpha no: -19.76   check: -0.9999999999999999
avrg alpha no: -19.69   check: -1.0
avrg alpha no: -19.84   check: -1.0

C TRIAL 3

---

0 beta: 0.35   avrg. a: 3.54
1 beta: 0.53   avrg. a: 3.54
2 beta: 0.68   avrg. a: 3.54
3 beta: 0.87   avrg. a: 3.54
4 beta: 1.12   avrg. a: 3.54
5 beta: 1.16   avrg. a: 3.54
6 beta: 1.24   avrg. a: 3.54
7 beta: 1.33   avrg. a: 3.54
8 beta: 1.27   avrg. a: 3.54
9 beta: 1.27   avrg. a: 3.54
10 beta: 1.15   avrg. a: 3.54
11 beta: 1.04   avrg. a: 3.54
12 beta: 1.24   avrg. a: 3.54
13 beta: 1.92   avrg. a: 3.54
14 beta: 2.39   avrg. a: 3.54
15 beta: 2.29   avrg. a: 3.54
16 beta: 1.27   avrg. a: 3.54
17 beta: 0.74   avrg. a: 3.54
18 beta: 0.96   avrg. a: 3.54
19 beta: -0.73   avrg. a: 3.54

avrg alpha high: -69.73   avrg alpha average: 14.41
avrg alpha high: -71.46   avrg alpha average: -3.7
avrg alpha high: -69.74   avrg alpha average: -6.24
avrg alpha high: -70.22   avrg alpha average: -7.06
avrg alpha high: -71.53   avrg alpha average: -7.22
avrg alpha high: -71.39   avrg alpha average: -7.42
avrg alpha high: -71.53   avrg alpha average: -7.56
avrg alpha high: -71.52   avrg alpha average: -7.66

```
avrg alpha high: -71.71    avrg alpha average: -7.71
avrg alpha high: -71.63    avrg alpha average: -7.79
avrg alpha high: -71.4     avrg alpha average: -7.87
avrg alpha high: -71.25    avrg alpha average: -7.96
avrg alpha high: -71.63    avrg alpha average: -7.95
avrg alpha high: -72.26    avrg alpha average: -7.89
avrg alpha high: -72.42    avrg alpha average: -7.87
avrg alpha high: -72.34    avrg alpha average: -7.89
avrg alpha high: -71.37    avrg alpha average: -8.03
avrg alpha high: -70.21    avrg alpha average: -8.2
avrg alpha high: -71.1     avrg alpha average: -8.09
avrg alpha high: -70.62    avrg alpha average: -8.16

avrg alpha no: -44.68      check: -1.0
avrg alpha no: -24.83      check: -1.0
avrg alpha no: -24.01      check: -1.0
avrg alpha no: -22.71      check: -1.0
avrg alpha no: -21.24      check: -1.0
avrg alpha no: -21.18      check: -1.0
avrg alpha no: -20.9       check: -1.0
avrg alpha no: -20.8       check: -1.0
avrg alpha no: -20.56      check: -1.0
avrg alpha no: -20.57      check: -1.0
avrg alpha no: -20.71      check: -1.0
avrg alpha no: -20.78      check: -0.9999999999999999
avrg alpha no: -20.4       check: -0.9999999999999999
avrg alpha no: -19.84      check: -1.0
avrg alpha no: -19.69      check: -0.9999999999999999
avrg alpha no: -19.76      check: -1.0
avrg alpha no: -20.59      check: -1.0
avrg alpha no: -21.58      check: -1.0
avrg alpha no: -20.79      check: -1.0
avrg alpha no: -21.21      check: -1.0
```

About
the Authors

LENANDLAR SINGH

Lenandlar Singh is Head of the Department of Computer Science at the University of Guyana. He graduated from the University of Guyana with a BSc (Distinction) in computer science, then completed a Post Graduate Diploma in Education (Distinction). He continues to mentor, supervise and enthuse students like Zach-Amaury Boufoy-Bastick through his dedicated teaching and motivating research interests in computer science. His main field of research is in internet computing and its applications. He has continued to pursue formal studies in e-governance in the Caribbean, and internet technologies in India. In 2004 he was awarded the j2ee technologies certificate by Tata Infotech, New Delhi.

lenandlar.singh@uog.edu.gy

ZACH-AMAURY BOUFOY-BASTICK

Zach-Amaury Boufoy-Bastick was educated in more than a dozen countries across the world – including North, South and Central America, the Caribbean, South-East Asia, the South Pacific, and his native region of Western Europe. He attended the University of the West Indies in Jamaica and the University of Guyana, and is currently studying at Université Paris IV Sorbonne. His pan-cultural and multi-national experience has engendered interests that straddle both the arts and sciences, resulting in his academic papers being published in both Journals of Philosophy and of Computing. His past research, designing socially appropriate interactive systems deploying assignments of human attributes, and his current research in innovations and controls on internet access, give technical under-pinning to his current interest to inform proactive international policies for computer-regulation of societies that protect freedoms of Internet access.

zach.bastick@gmail.com

Modelling Integrated Socio-technical Feedback Systems